The

SCOUSERS

by

Doreen M. Doyle

with

Joe Giambrone

Publisher

Indies United Publishing House LLC.

P.O. Box 3071

Quincy, IL 62305-3071

indiesunited.net

*

Paperback Version

Available in e-book, paperback, and hardcover.

*

Paperback

ISBN13: 978-1-64456-086-0

Hardcover

ISBN13: 978-1-64456-087-7

EPUB

ISBN13: 978-1-64456-088-4

MOBI

ASIN: B0817KWHL8

Photo credits: Peter Whitney, Tom Whitney, Gladys Whitney, Lucy Doyle, Doreen Doyle and Joe Giambrone.

Front Cover: Gladys Whitney on the rubble of her bombed house with little Jeanie; Lucy pushing three grandchildren in a cart; and young Doreen, Jean, and Frank Doyle in 1945.

Back Cover: Tom Whitney standing on the deck of the HMS. *Starling*, a "submarine killer," credit Peter Whitney.

Editor: Clare Coombes, *Liverpool Editing Co.*

Table of Contents

Foreword

This book tells one family's struggle during and after World War Two. All the information is true, as best as we can recall. We kept the details as accurate as we were able to research.

Some of the scenes utilize creative non-fiction to try and bring the time period to life.

There were many thousands, perhaps millions of stories of sheer grit during World War Two. This was our family's.

To all those who struggled so hard to survive against all the odds: *Rest in Peace.*

Acknowledgments

To Eileen Powell, my Aunty, who kept these moments alive for us. She talked around her kitchen fire at 11 Sefton Grove, Aigburth, Liverpool, for many years. I would like to offer her a big thank you in Heaven for passing down these family stories to me.

To Peter Whitney, my cousin, the baby born November 2nd 1936, who spent endless hours searching through his Dad's old letters and effects. He provided so much priceless information.

To my son Joe, who despite being legally blind, has spent untold hours helping me get my book ready to publish.

To all of the brave Scousers who fought so hard and suffered so much during this most terrible time in British history: "Yer all right, all of yis!"

Part of the proceeds from this book will be shared with the Liverpool *Salvation Army* and the *Liverpool Catholic Charities*. Without them both we most certainly would have starved to death.

-*Doreen M. Doyle*

Doreen & Joe, 1967 | credit: Doreen Doyle

Chapter One

Winter of 1936

T he Whitneys were a happy loving family from the Aigburth and Dingle area of Liverpool. There were two boys and three girls in the family. Tom was the eldest, then came Eileen, then Lucy (my Mum), then Agnes whom we all called Nell, and Jack, the baby.

My Aunt Gladys and Uncle Tom lived in the Dingle section of Liverpool, which is known as Liverpool-8.

Most streets consisted of terraced houses, some with a little front garden, most had two or three bedrooms. Some featured inside toilets, a typical middle class part of the city. Gladys' house on Woodruff Street was a small three-up two-down house with no inside bathroom. Most middle class houses did not have inside bathrooms until after World War Two. It was a nicely kept street with spotless front steps. Back then, everyone scrubbed their front steps each morning.

The windows on the street were spotless. People took great pride in cleaning them every week. Window cleaners came around, and most people had them do the outside. These were very reasonable with the cost. The mums did the insides of the windows. Everyone hung out the washing on clotheslines, then finished drying it on the maiden in front of the fire.

Some houses had damp spots in the walls. None had central heating back then, but overall the houses on Woodruff Street were classic middle class homes, nice and comfortable.

The Whitneys were a close-knit family, even though Tom was sent away for most of the war. Prior to that, he served in the Merchant Navy.

My Aunty Gladys showed great strength in the years leading up to the war, caring for her family and friends. With her husband Tom Whitney away at sea, she faced crises at home against pneumonia and diphtheria, an epidemic sweeping across the country. It was known as *the Plague Among Children.*

Gladys would hug her two-year-old, Tommy, a little bit tighter each night.

When Tom Whitney returned home on leave, they would go to the local pub and join the rest of the family in singalongs.

Gladys had three sisters who gladly watched little Tommy for her. Her sister Lily had volunteered that night to watch the toddler. Gladys, meanwhile, was almost due with her second baby.

As Tom and Gladys strolled back home after a singing session at the *Albert* on Lark lane in Aigburth, she began to feel sharp stabbing pains down her spine.

"Tom, I think I may be starting off a bit early," she announced, pausing to catch her breath.

"Oh shite!" he said. "Let's get you home then."

As they arrived at their house, her pains came on stronger and closer together. Gladys' matinee coats and booties were laid out, ready for the baby's arrival.

Gladys Whitney | credit: Peter Whitney

Tom sat her carefully onto the couch. "I'll go tell Mrs. Brown!"

Mrs. Brown placed her medical bag on the table alongside her knitting, which she took to each delivery to pass the time. She examined Gladys, while Gladys' sister Lily stayed on to see if she could be of help.

"Well, love," she Mrs. B., timing the contractions. "It won't be a very long night." A plump little Irish lady, she loved delivering new lives into the world. Mrs. Brown sat quietly by the bed, knitting an Aran jacket for her granddaughter.

Gladys' new baby arrived about three hours after they had returned from the pub, giving Mrs. Brown plenty of time to finish a sleeve on the lovely jacket she was knitting.

Tom paced the kitchen, puffing a cigarette and listening to the wireless. At one in the morning, the baby arrived and screeched his little head off.

Mrs. Brown caught Tom to announce, "Oh another lovely little lad yer got here, just gorgeous."

She weighed him, cut the cord, and placed him onto the scale. "A good weight too, eight-pounds four-ounces. What you gonna call him?"

"Peter," Tom replied.

Tom Whitney | credit: Peter Whitney

"Yeah. Peter," said Gladys, her exhausted face shining with happiness. "Ooh God, he's just perfect. Look at those little hands, Tom." She cried with joy.

Lily left early the next morning to tell the

family of the arrival of Peter.

Peter came on a treat, and in no time he was crawling around the house. At nine months he was walking. He and his brother Tommy became the little men of the house.

Tom had recently joined the Merchant Navy and was away for several months.

Gladys received a letter saying Tom would be coming home on leave, and she was so excited. It had been difficult alone with her two little lads to care for. Gladys rushed to the butcher to buy meat to cook Scouse, Tom's favorite meal. She could almost taste the stew, made with mutton, potatoes, carrots and onions, a cheap but satisfying dish. She always cooked Scouse for special occasions. They all loved it, and often dunked in buttered bread. Her heart leapt at the thought of her husband coming home on leave and his face when she placed the steaming dish in front of him to inhale, back with home comforts.

Wrapping her threadbare coat around tightly, she tried to keep warm in the biting winds.

Inside the butcher's Gladys met up with Mrs. Seddon, her neighbor from up the street. They had lived near each other for years, sharing the holidays and kids' birthday parties.

Mrs. Seddon was two years older than Gladys, with platinum blonde hair, always done up lovely on top of her head in curls. She was a pretty lady and talked quickly, but always sweet to everyone.

"How's your little Tommy doing, Glad?"

"Smashing. He's talking up a storm and knows all our names, and shouts Dada all the time. Don't yer, lad?" Gladys rubbed the top of Tommy's head.

Mrs. Seddon asked, "Does Peter sleep good for ya, love?"

"Oh yeah. He's a proper good little lad."

The butcher wrapped Gladys a chuck steak. Steak was an expensive cut of meat, but it was for Tom's arrival back home.

"No worries with 'im," said Gladys.

They were both avoiding the subject that was on every mums' mind these days.

Gladys said, "Did you hear about Mary Brown from Denton Street? Her little lad died on Tuesday from diphtheria. He was only sick a few weeks."

"It's awful how many this is taking," said Mrs Seddon. "That's the third one I've heard of this week."

"Terrible."

They shook their heads and looked down into Peter's pram, as he gurgled happily.

Gladys headed off toward the greengrocer's. Along the way, she saw Frances Roberts stepping off the tram in front of *Sturla's* department store. Tears ran from her dark brown eyes, her face pale against the dark curls. The two ladies had been friends for years with many dances and trips to Blackpool behind them.

Frances caught sight of Gladys and shouted as she ran towards her, "My little lad, Gladys, my little lad!"

"Dear God," said Gladys, embracing Frances, who was soaked through. "I'm so sorry, love."

They sobbed and held onto each other.

"Come home with me for a cup of tea."

Frances slumped against Gladys. She'd spent two sleepless nights in Smithdown Road Hospital.

They rushed back home in the deluge, Gladys pushing the pram through the storm. Her tattered old coat sopped up a cloud's worth. Lifting little Tommy from his seat on Peters pram, his head felt warm. To calm her fears, she rubbed his hair and dried him off, then dressed him in dry clothes.

Frances dropped quietly into the easy chair as Gladys lit the fire. They removed their wet coats and shoes and shivered in the drafty house.

Gladys heated the kettle on the stove and they had a good long talk about what Fran should do next. Fran had to arrange a coffin for her little lad, then sort out the funeral costs.

Gladys advised her to see the funeral director on Park Road. He was known to arrange for people to pay the costs back over time. Frances hadn't seen her other boy, Brian, in two days. She had slept in the chair of the hospital room. Now her neck and back were killing her, from sleeping in that uncomfortable chair.

Gladys comforted Frances. "You are strong, love, remember." Gladys kissed Frances goodbye.

Neighbours on Briarwood Road had taken care of little Brian while Fran was at the hospital with her sick boy.

Gladys shut the door, and it seemed like everyone knew of a baby dying from one of those dreaded sicknesses. Little Tommy remained asleep, his forehead warmer than expected. Gladys tried not to fret and turned on the radio to distract herself, checking her son's temperature occasionally.

There was more talk of war in Europe. The BBC reported on the unrest. *Jesus I hope we don't get dragged into it*, she thought.

A sudden knock at the front door revealed Lucy and Nellie, her two Sisters-In-Law. They often visited for lunch or just a cup of tea when the kids went to bed.

"I'm worried about little Tommy," Gladys confided in them.

The pair advised her to phone Doctor Roberts from a neighbor's house. She made the call, and the doctor agreed to come out the next morning.

In the time before the NHS, doctors often took on poor patients free of charge.

With help from her Sisters-In-Law, Aunty Gladys prepared a bath for two-year-old Tommy. Lucy fed little Peter. Nell cleared out old ashes and lit a new fire.

Tommy's cough sounded chesty as she lifted him. Rubbing *Vicks* on his chest seemed to help a bit. Home remedies often included *Vicks*.

The next morning, little Tommy seemed to have perked up. Gladys put *Vicks* in boiling water and a towel over his head for a few minutes. His breathing started to improve.

A familiar voice called in, "Anybody home here?"

Gladys dropped her spoon, as she had just started the Scouse. and she ran to her husband.

Tom stood in the doorway, looking stunning in

his navy uniform.

"Oh love, I'm so glad to see you!" As she hugged him, the tension of little Tommy's illness seemed to seep out of her bones.

Tom lifted her and planted a big kiss on her lips. "Where's me little lads?"

Little Tommy was asleep in his pram by the fire. In all the commotion, he woke up. "Dada!" he said.

Tom scooped him up.

"Here I am, lad. Yer dad is 'ome!"

Tom Whitney sat with his lads on his knee, so happy to be back home.

Gladys could smell the sea on him.

As Gladys unpacked a delicate silk scarf, Tom laughed with delight. The scarf was purple and pink with bits of pale green here and there on the pattern. He showed her his latest photos from traveling in the Merchant Navy. Tom was such a handsome man with his lush black hair and brown eyes. He had traveled to Gibraltar and Malta, where he loved the people he had met. He told Gladys they were wonderful and friendly.

"Smashing that, Tom. I've made you a Scouse for tea."

"I've been dying for a good plate of real Scouse. It's shite the stuff they feed us on board. I've missed your cooking, love."

Tom wolfed down his tea, and Gladys considered how to tell him how worried she was about Tommy. Peter was thriving, no worries with him, but Tommy wasn't feeling well at all.

"Everything OK?" said Tom, his fork paused halfway to his mouth.

Gladys pushed food around on her plate. "Tommy hasn't been too well. The doctor is coming out tomorrow."

Little Tommy coughed out loudly, a rattling sound in his chest.

Tom looked over. "He doesn't sound too well, love." His brow furrowed, he placed down his knife and fork and scraped back his chair.

"I know. He has a bit of a bad chest. I've been rubbing the *Vicks* in. It's 'elping a bit."

"I'll watch him 'til the doctor comes," said Tom. "You get some rest."

Gladys felt exhausted from caring for Tommy and the new baby as well. When the doctor arrived, Gladys awoke from dozing in the chair.

Doctor Roberts examined little Tommy, and he said that they had nothing to worry about.

Relieved, Gladys started to clean up the back kitchen. Tom entertained the boy, crawling across the floor as a horsey. Little Tommy screeched with delight.

Gladys dressed little Tommy and Peter warmly, and they took off round to Tom's parents' house, a couple of miles down Park Road to Aigburth Road, then up Lark Lane to Bickerton Street. Park Road was very busy back in the '30s with family-owned businesses and lots of groups of neighbours gathered on corners catching up with the local news.

Aigburth Road wasn't quite as busy as Park Road. A lovely "Chippy" sat halfway down between Park Road and Lark Lane. The fantastic smells of the fresh cod and chips would make your tummy rumble as you walked past.

Lark Lane was a family area. Small shops catered to just about everything anyone would need, from new carpets to potatoes. In the middle of the block sat the clinic all the locals went to, from babies receiving our dried milk to pre-teens getting our cod liver oil and orange juice.

Tom Whitney's mum hugged him tightly. His dad shook his hand firmly, beaming at his returned son.

Tom's kid brother, Jack, wanted to know, "What's been happening on the ships?"

Tom described all his training on the HMS *Drake* in the Merchant Navy. He was now trained as a gun layer spotting targets from a distance.

Tom quizzed Jack. "How yer doing in school, our kid?" Jack had been taking classes for extra credits.

"Alright," said Jack. "One year left, and I'll be looking for a good job."

Tom's sister Eileen entered with her two little

ones. Everyone caught up with the latest.

Jack Whitney at 15 | credit: Peter Whitney

Tom patted the top of Jack's head and messed up his hair. Their Mum served tea with digestive biscuits. They slurped and crunched hungrily in the small sitting room.

"Lovely treat that, Mam," said Tom. How's work, Dad?"

"Not bad, lad," said his Dad. Tom's father worked down in the mines of Wales. He would take the train in each Sunday night, work all week, sleep in a boarding house close by, and then return home to Liverpool late on Friday. His lungs steadily worsened from inhaling coal dust.

"We're lucky to 'ave jobs nowadays with all this bleeding talk of war," Tom said.

"Not in front of the kids, love," his Mum whispered.

"Alright, Ma," said Tom. "Time we get 'ome now." Tom's Mum and Dad got very emotional as he left, not knowing when they would see him again. Eileen seemed upset as well, choking back tears as she kissed him and the kids and Gladys goodbye.

Gladys checked on Little Tommy as they turned the corner toward the shops. He didn't seem strong at all, and he sounded chesty.

Gladys planned to pick up an ox's heart for

Sunday's dinner. The butcher's was mobbed as usual. The shop sold dirt-cheap meat that smelled off. Anyone who bought it, and plenty did, would rub salt to get rid of the stench. No one could remember anyone actually getting ill. The meats were laid out in the front window, often covered in flies.

Tom bought an ox's heart for five bob, and away home they went. Gladys caught the scent of batter and vinegar from the Chippy on Park Road and her stomach rumbled.

"You fancy fish and chips, Tom?"

"Yeah. That'll be smashing." They headed inside with the pram and ordered tea.

The Park Road Chippy was a nice clean place. Their food was delicious, and even better it was affordable. The restaurant had white tiles up the walls and huge vats of oil to cook the fish and chips. Your mouth would water as you waited for your order.

Luckily, the Park Road Chippy never was bombed during WW2. However, lots of local shops nearby were.

Gladys felt Tommy's forehead as the fish fried. "Does he feel a bit warm to you?"

Tommy inspected his son. "Yeah. Just a bit."

"I'll rub some more *Vicks* on his chest to help him sleep. It 'elps a lot," Gladys decided.

After they devoured the chippy tea, Gladys put little Tommy back down for the night and sang him to sleep. The boy's eyelids fluttered and closed.

She fed and bathed little Peter and put him down for the night in his Pram by the fire. After he'd nodded off, they turned on the BBC. The broadcast talked only about war in Europe.

"It's scary, don't you think, Tom?"

"Yeah. But it's not coming here, love. Trust me on that."

Tom reassured her as he packed his things to return to his ship and train off the coast of Scotland. He knew how scared Gladys would be alone with the kids.

Tom's mate arrived at the house in the morning. Tom kissed Gladys goodbye, and the men trotted off to catch the tram to Dock Road. He would be gone for three or four months.

Little Tommy awoke with coughs and a rattling in his throat. Difficulty breathing, he struggled to gulp in air.

Gladys rushed across to the neighbour's and phoned up Doctor Roberts again. When Roberts arrived with his kit bag, Gladys could see the deep lines etched into his face.

"He's got worse, Doctor," she said.

The Doctor had been dealing with so many sick children in the area. "Well, let's take another look then." He checked little Tommy's lungs with his stethoscope.

Gladys watched his face cloud over.

"Mmm," he said. "I think I'll send you down to Smithdown Road for an X-ray. I don't like the sound of them."

Gladys started to panic. "Will he be okay, Doctor?"

"Oh, don't worry. Once we get the X-ray we can

get him onto some good cough medicine."

He wrote her a script and passed it over. His hand patted her shoulder. "Take him this afternoon. Best not to wait with matters like this."

My Aunty Gladys quickly prepared jam butties and filled a milk bottle with water in case they had to wait. She changed little Tommy. He seemed lethargic, not his feisty usual self at all. She ran them up Park Road to catch the tram to Smithdown Road Hospital. As it clattered along the tracks, Gladys tried to calm herself, but her chest remained tight with worry, her mouth dry with fear.

It was an awful long walk to reach the hospital. Little Tommy cried, sitting on the little seat on the front of the pram.

As she filled out the hospital forms, Tommy screamed. She tried to get him to eat.

Another mum saw that Gladys was overwhelmed with Tommy's crying. So, she offered to feed little Peter. Gladys was so relieved to get a helper.

Eventually, they were called into the X-ray

department's waiting room.

"Don't cry, lad," Gladys whispered as they took him in for his X-ray. "Nearly done. Such a brave little lad, aren't yer?"

The orderlies wheeled little Tommy in, as he screamed with fear. The nurse holding him down on the stretcher tried to comfort him. Gladys was heartbroken, as she remained out in the waiting room.

She knew the X-ray would cost them a small fortune, but it was desperately needed.

"We'll contact your doctor with the results," the technician told her.

Gladys thanked them and headed for the door and the long walk back down Smithdown Road.

Poor little Tommy cried through the night. Gladys poured *Vicks* into hot water and placed a towel over his head, so he would breathe in the fumes. If only he could cough it all out, he would feel so much better. His little lungs seemed to fill with phlegm.

The next morning Gladys telephoned the doctor from her neighbor's house, frantic over how sick Tommy had become in the night. After what seemed an eternity, Doctor Roberts came on the phone and listened to Gladys explain how everything had gotten worse.

"I have an ambulance on its way," he told her. "We will be admitting him. He has to go right into an oxygen tent to help him breathe."

Gladys's heart pounded like it would rip out of her chest. "He'll be OK, won't he, doctor?"

"We'll do everything we can for him."

Gladys packed up baby supplies and Tommy's teddy bear he'd been given last Christmas.

Mrs. Seddon, their kindly neighbour, offered to watch baby Peter while Gladys went to hospital with Tommy.

"Don't cry, darlin'. You'll be better soon!" she told her son, even as her own tears clouded her vision.

The ambulance pulled up. In marched two attendants with a stretcher. They carried little Tommy out and into the ambulance.

"Oh, God. I wish Tom was here." Gladys cried as

she climbed into the ambulance, but there was no way
of getting in touch with Tom. He was out on a ship in
the ocean somewhere. Eventually, they did get a
message to Tom.

The ambulance attendants placed an oxygen
mask on little Tommy's tired face. Gladys held his tiny
hand for the whole trip.

On arrival, they rushed him inside and right up
into a room with an oxygen tent. The nurses told
Gladys she could stay with him, and she sat in a chair
by Tommy's side.

For two whole days she remained with him.
Word spread back through the family. Neighbors had
seen the ambulance. While Gladys waited by Tommy's
oxygen tent, a five-year-old girl in the bed opposite,
and a one-year-old boy further down the ward both
died from pneumonia.

The grief of the deceased children's families
was unbearable. They broke down and wailed on the
ward. The sounds of the anguish were everywhere.
Gladys hoped to God that her little lad wouldn't end up

like them. She occupied herself by knitting for baby Peter, but her hands shook as she watched her son struggle to take each breath.

Her Mam brought in tea and ham butties. Gladys lived on an occasional cup of tea and some digestive biscuits. As she nodded off from exhaustion, she heard Tommy scream out. His chest sounded so phlegmy he couldn't breathe any longer.

"Nurse!" she shouted. "Nurse!"

Little Tommy lay still, his eyes staring up at his Mum.

A doctor came in and listened to his lungs.

"I'm very sorry," he said to Gladys, his face grave. "He is dying."

"Oh, God no!"

She broke down and fell to her knees.

"Please say you're wrong."

The nurses put their arms around her asking how they could contact her family.

"Let me hold him," she asked. "Let me hold him one last time."

They lifted the oxygen tent flap and Gladys scooped his little frail body up in her arms.

"You're such a brave lad," she told Tommy. "Mam and Dad love yer." She kissed him all over his tiny face, and he suddenly went limp.

Gladys's Mam ran into the room. Lucy and Nell followed along with Tom's Mam. The family held each other, sobbing and trying to find some comfort.

Little Tommy was dead, just over two-years old. The tragic story of little Tommy's death was often spoken about within the family, except by Aunty Gladys, who found it hard to even say his name for the rest of her life.

During that time period, one in every 20 children died of one of the dreaded diseases. After World War Two broke out, Britain began to immunize the population against them. Within a few years they were eradicated. Life expectancy rose and children were no longer dying of diphtheria.

The immunization programme was a huge success and saved thousands of lives. What prompted the government to begin the immunizations was the fact that people would be in such close proximity during the war in the air raid shelters. Also, the newspapers reported on the successes that the USA and Canada were having with similar programmes.

In 1928, A Scottish scientist, Sir Alexander Fleming discovered penicillin. It was still very difficult to manufacture on a large scale. Consequently, it was not used widely until 1940. Today we take for granted the use of antibiotics, however during the 1930s one in every 20 children under two-years old died of diseases we can easily cure today.

Chapter Two

The Funeral, 1937

Gladys Whitney said, "He's in a better place I just know it." It was a terrible time for the entire familiy.

"Yer right, love." Everyone agreed.

"He's a little angel now."

They crammed into Tom and Gladys' front parlour, not enough chairs for everyone to sit. Most of the family held onto each other weeping at the devastating news of little Tommy's death. Neighbours brought tins of biscuits and made pots of tea. The fire roared up the chimney. Shadows from the fire bounced off the walls, it was quite hot in the front parlour.

The Merchant Navy arranged for Tom Whitney

to catch a train home in an hour upon hearing the bad news. He arrived at Lime Street station at 2am. No trams ran at that hour, and so he ran home. Gladys hadn't slept in days. Her complexion was ghostly and her face streaked with tears.

Tom rushed in. "Oh God, love."

Gladys's Mum, who had been staying with her, stood up and went to make a pot of tea, leaving the couple to talk. Usually a formidable woman, with not a hair out of place, she too looked wiped out by the tragedy.

Tom took her seat beside Gladys.

Gladys said. "The ozzy wanted me to get the coffin."

Tom bowed his head, his arm around her shoulder. "Right then. We'll go up the funeral place up on Park Road as soon as they open."

The funeral home had a pleasant private room with stained glass windows and bright sunlight streaming through. The funeral director, Mr. O'Hara, offered his condolences, as he showed Gladys and Tom inside.

Gladys inspected all the tiny coffins on display. She felt drawn to a hazel pine one with white handles.

Mr. O'Hara explained, "You pick out which coffin you want your little lad buried in, and I'll make all the arrangements then for his funeral."

Mr. O'Hara was a much loved member of the community, despite the fact most of the women towered over him. His kindness made him huge in everyone's eyes.

"That one," said Gladys finally, lightly touching the white handle with her finger. "We want to give him the very best send off we can."

Tom grabbed her hand and kissed it. "Then we'll 'ave that one, love."

Most people of the area had very little money to pay for a funeral. They knew that Mr. O'Hara would work with them, and they would pay just a few shillings per week over several years.

Mr. O'Hara went over his numbers. "It will all cost two pound 17 shillings and six pence," he said.

His throat coughed slightly before adding, "That's the best I can do, sorry. That's a solid hazel pine chest coffin, and very high quality."

Tom and Gladys trudged back home at a slow pace. Neither could talk. Their silence was surrounded by the bustle of the city. Park Road was busy as usual, people shopping for groceries. Most had to shop daily, as very few owned refrigerators. Those who could afford it bought pies from the cake shops along the street, or sausage rolls, or fish and chips.

The two endured the next two days before the funeral in much the same way, lost in their thoughts of little Tommy. Loving neighbors sent pans of steaming stew and soup.

Gladys got some comfort holding onto baby Peter, but her heart was broken. So was Tom's.

The morning of the funeral was cold and drizzly. Tom and Gladys felt even worse for it.

Mr. McGee, their friend neighbour from down the street, drove them to Toxteth Park Cemetery. The cost of the car to bring little Tommy's coffin was a small fortune to them.

The remainder of the family walked or arrived by tram.

Gladys floated around in a daze. During the funeral service Gladys and Tom wept openly. Prayers and music were mildly comforting, but the holes in their hearts from the loss of little Tommy never filled again.

Gladys' sisters made them sardine butties for lunch after the funeral service, and a plate of queen cakes with cream on top.

The family returned to Tom and Gladys' house on Woodruff Street.

Tom only had leave for 48 hours, and then it was back to the HMS *Drake* to finish his training. After he said goodbye, Gladys sobbed for hours.

Nell and Lucy stayed with her, making cups of tea and bringing small spoonfuls of soup to her lips. She had to regain her strength, which grief had stolen from her. The Sisters-In-Law cleaned the little house from top to bottom, changed baby Peter, and eventually tucked Gladys into bed.

Chapter Three

Lucy & Herbert

Despite her broken heart, Gladys kept on, and she waited for Tom's return, who was due back again around Christmas.

Lucy, my Mum, and her sister Nell visited Gladys regularly. Lucy told of her new job in *Woolworth's*. It had only recently opened and everyone loved shopping there, as it had tons of small affordable items, nail polish, scarves, stockings, birthday and other cards, which were a hit at that time. People spent hours shopping in this new type of store, its counters filled with all types of merchandise, from socks to perfume and make-up.

Nell worked at the local green grocery store, selling fruit and vegetables. She loved chatting with customers.

Gladys was glad of the distractions their chatter brought.

Lucy showed off her finely polished nails. "You have to have nice hands to work on the counter. I've got a new fella by the way." Her eyes danced with excitement. "Met him in Sefton Park. He plays the guitar. We all sat on the grass while he sang to us and played songs. I couldn't keep me eyes off him."

Gladys grinned widely. "What's the lad's name?"

"Herby. Herby Doyle from the Vale."

Gladys shifted back. "Oh that's a dead posh neighborhood, Aigburth Vale."

Lucy nodded. "He's a sewing machine mechanic. A proper good job."

"When you seeing him again?" asked Gladys.

"Saturday. We're all going the park, a gang of us, to 'ave a singalong."

On Saturday afternoon Gladys prepared to meet Lucy's new boyfriend. She needed a night of music and revelry to take her mind off everything. Putting her hair up in clips, it flowed nicely when she combed it out, soft under her fingers.

Tom had returned on leave again, and it was a proper date night. Lucy, Gladys, and Tom gathered at the Albert Hotel on Lark Lane for a few drinks. The pub was always warm and lively and had little areas separated out with roaring fires in each one. The sound of laughter spilled out from the bar, alongside the melodic tones of a piano being played in the corner.

Lucy's new boyfriend, Herby, had brought along his guitar. After they met him, he approached the piano player, Eddie Hughes.

"Okay if I join in, lad?" he asked. Herby held his guitar up with a hopeful expression on his face.

"Sure," came the reply. The two musicians began playing what would become a regular night out for years to come. Herby never had to pay for his ale again, due to the crowds he brought into the pub.

Gladys and Tom were impressed with Lucy's

date, and they told her so. She was quite relieved now that she had fallen for Herbert.

Instead of going to Sefton Park for a singalong, they all decided it was much nicer and warmer at the Albert. Everyone sang to the guitar and piano in the pub.

Eileen Powell, my Aunty | credit: Doreen Doyle

Herbert and Lucy finished playing a rendition of *We are Wanderers of the Wasteland*, a country song that everyone knew. The entire pub sang with them.

Eileen and her husband, also named Tom, would often come into the pub. A surprisingly good singer, my Aunty Eileen sang *My Happiness* with Herby Doyle on guitar and Eddie Hughes on the piano. You could hear a pin drop while she performed. The men stopped sipping their pints of bitter and the women paused over sherries and wine.

Chapter Four

New Brighton Trip

Summer of 1938, the weather forecast was for a warm, sunny weekend. Lucy and Eileen thought it would be a great day out to New Brighton Baths for a swim. New Brighton was a stunning new place for a day out, with a huge pool and seating all around. It had snack bars, diving boards, and was just a lovely spot to spend the day. Lucy had a day off from *Woolworths*, and Nell had the day off from her greengrocer's. They would all meet up at the Pier Head to take the ferry across the Mersey to New Brighton.

Gladys arrived first and she fed little Peter, who was just over a year-old.

Lucy and Eileen arrived shortly after. Eileen

had bought little Eil and Fred a swimming cozzy each, so the two kids could splash around in the pool. The children couldn't stop smiling as they queued up for the ferry.

The Mums had packed butties, jam, *Spam*, and egg ones. "That should do us all day," said Eileen.

The breeze from off the river felt heavenly, as they stood in the queue for the next ferry. The cobblestones glistened in the sun. The *Royal Liver Building* stood proudly, with its Liver Birds perched on top.

"Lovely day, isn't it, Glad?" Lucy said. "All ready to go?"

"Aye," said Gladys. "The next ferry sails at ten. Where's Nell?"

"She hadn't finished doing her hair," said Lucy. "She should be on the next tram."

That tram pulled up and Nell jumped off, out of breath. "Sorry. Couldn't find me other shoe."

They all burst out laughing. "Yer soft mare," said Eileen. "You'd lose yer ed if it wasn't screwed on."

Nell's hair was done up lovely with ringlets of curls. With her slim figure, she looked like a model.

They all piled onto the ferry, and the kids ran around, their feet thundering across the boards.

The vessel, which was the main route for many between Liverpool and the Wirral, steamed straight across the murky river with a plume of smoke.

The three little cousins Fred, Eileen, and Peter had a great time.

"Be careful you two!" Eileen shouted at her kids as they charged past in a game of hide and seek.

Little Peter watched his cousins from his pram, gurgling and smiling.

They soon reached the New Brighton Baths. Through the turnstiles and inside, they admired the magnificent Art Deco and high diving boards. The salty sea air mixed with their delicious sandwiches, and made for a perfect summer day out.

"Oh Christ!" Gladys announced. "I forgot to pack the suntan lotion."

Lucy stepped up. "I've got some, Glad. I don't

need any premature wrinkles."

The two giggled, and then they smothered the children with lotion. The Mums tucked their frocks up into the legs of their knickers. They held the little ones in the pool, splashing and screeching through the afternoon. After a few hours the kids tired.

Gladys shouted, "Come on you lot. We're 'avin a picnic over 'ere. Get yourselves some butties."

Eileen brought a flask of hot tea and poured it carefully, with steam rising from the paper cups.

Lucy took some gratefully and toasted with her cup. Her legs already sun-kissed, she stretched them out. "This has been a smashing day. I've got a good tan going."

Nellie concurred. "Oh aye, yeah. Me legs are gettin' nice and brown too. I've been sunnin' them all morning." She pulled her frock up to show off her tan lines.

"Wow, brown as a berry," said Gladys.

After lunch, the kids started pushing each other and shouting. The Mums decided to take a walk along the waterfront by the Mersey. Little Fred's legs gave out first. Gladys sat them on the seat at the front of her pram.

Several ships sailed down the river, so the kids were excited to watch them. It was a clear, sunny day, with blue skies and no clouds in sight. One of the kids spotted an ice cream van and begged to have one.

Eileen checked her purse. "You can 'ave one between yers." She picked a huge orange lolly ice for them to share.

Their group slowly trekked back toward the pier, eventually resting on benches and the freshly cut grass

Nell admired the sleeping infant. "What a good baby little Peter is. Not a bit of trouble."

"I know," said Gladys. "He loves to be out and about."

The waves of the Mersey rocked them, and then they caught the clattering tram back home to south Liverpool. These lovely days out were so rare for the family that they talked about them for the next fifteen years.

After I turned 12-years old we moved neighbourhoods. We lived 8-miles away. So, I didn't visit my Aunty Eileen as often, although I would occasionally stop by her house. By the time I reached 15, my friends took up much more of my life.

Chapter Five

Ray's Sale

Word spread like wildfire that *Ray's*, the dish shop located in the middle of Park Road, was having its big annual sale. Every year they sold off discontinued China and sets with chipped or cracked dishes at a fraction of the original cost. This was the only chance my Mum, Lucy, her sisters Eileen and Nell, and her Sister-In-Law Gladys, had to purchase decent dishes.

They were salivating at the chance for a big score and agreed to work in unison to grab the right dishes to match each other.

When they arrived early on the day of the sale there was already a massive queue.

"Jesus!" said Aunty Eileen. "You would think

they were giving it away!"

The women quickly shuffled to their spot at the back of the queue, ready to charge inside. The doors opened with a mad rush. Boxes all over the shop were filled with slightly damaged plates.

Without a pram or little ones to hold her back, Lucy raced over to the best China she could grab. Lucy jogged back and found Gladys. "'ere, love! Isn't this the one you wanted?" She plonked a fancy white sugar bowl atop the pram's cover.

Eileen shouted back over the roar, "Grab that other big plate, Lu!"

Lucy snatched it just before an older lady could get her hands on it. They looked at one another, eyes narrowed, before bursting out laughing.

By the time the sale had finished they were knackered.

Lucy collected four dinner plates and six China cups and was thrilled to bits. Gladys had found a crystal sugar bowl as well as a milk jug. They both clutched their possessions close to their chests and beamed at each other as they paid.

Lucy calmed from all that Adrenalin. "Let's pick up some nice pork pies at *Sayers* for lunch."

"Marvelous," said Gladys, excited for a treat at the cake shop.

The smell of freshly baked bread hit their nostrils as they walked in, alongside the sweet scent of cakes and the savoury items that made their stomachs rumble.

The family returned to Gladys' house, where she made them a pot of tea and brought out the pickled onions to eat with the pies. The sharp flavors were a welcome addition.

Eileen had bought creme cakes, which Lucy devoured.

"That was bloody lovely," said Lu, as she wiped cream from her face.

"Mmm," the other two piped in.

These shared lunches gave them all abundant chances to stay up on each other's lives. Aunty Eileen had been planning a cousins' birthday party, and my

Aunty Nell repeated the stories from her customers at the grocer's. Then there was a neighbour who had recently lost a baby, or another who had suddenly got a new job. They gossiped for hours.

Chapter Six

Lucy & Herby's Wedding

I t was 1939 and Lucy's big Wedding Day. Lucy ran around getting ready to wear her new wedding suit, which was made of a lovely silk material. It felt beautiful to slide your hand down, far different from the cotton uniforms she wore to work in *Woolworths*. In pastel beige, it matched her new hat and made up a simple, elegant outfit. Lucy had placed the posh outfit on hold for nine months and paid off the final two shillings just the Tuesday before.

"Keep your arms covered," said Lucy's Dad, who was very strict on the girls. They were forbidden to show bare skin in his house.

"Okay, Dad."

The girls wore scarves to cover their heads

when they went out and long sleeves most of the time.

Mums in our family didn't wear bathing suits, and so they would tuck their dresses up into their knickers, only exposing from the knee down. It was another twenty-five years before our girls started wearing bikinis. My Grandad was very old fashioned with what he allowed, but he meant well.

Lucy and Nell dressed up lovely with fancy hats that they had picked up last Friday. Lucy's hat had an elegant feather. Nell's lavender hat matched her white silk suit. Nell stood as Lucy's Matron of Honor, quite a heavy role for a seventeen-year-old, and she was thrilled to bits.

Jack Whitney dressed finely 'in Tom's pants and suit jacket. He looked so grown up in the Navy sports jacket with gray flannel pants. Jack was fifteen now and growing so quickly. His birthday was in a few weeks, and he was so excited that he could legally drink down at the pub.

Everyone wore their finest.

Herby Doyle was a protestant. Lucy's parents

didn't mind that Herby was protestant, despite the fact they were Irish Catholics. The old crotchety Catholic priest, however, wouldn't allow them to marry in front of the altar.

The old church had a lovely smell of incense burning. It featured three altars, the large main one, and two off to the side.

The Priest prayed in Latin after he married my Mum and Dad. Lucy and her sister Nell joined in. A neighbourhood lady named Phyllis played the organ as they emerged from church newly married.

Lucy's wedding party moved back to her Mam's house on Bickerton Street. The ten guests crammed into the front parlour. Lucy's Mam had spent weeks sewing new slip covers for her shabby furniture, and now it looked lovely. She even brought two bunches of spring flowers into the room, so it was all decked out.

"Lovely ham that is, Lu," said Nell. "Yer gettin' sent off in style."

"I am. Mam and Dad 'ave gone all out. Even a cake from Sayers." A double-layer 12-inch round cake, with marzipan and icing nicely decorated, strawberry shortcake inside with fresh strawberries and whipped cream, an exceptional real treat for everyone. On top were tiny statuettes of a bride and groom.

Lucy's Wedding | credit: Doreen Doyle

The two newlyweds rented a small house not far from Lucy's brother Tom Whitney and his wife Gladys. This was in the heart of Liverpool on

Wellington Road. A small two-up two-down house
built of brick, no hot water or inside toilet, but it was a
comfortable place to start married life.

Herby Doyle, my Dad, enlisted in the Scottish
Guards. He left for training down in London shortly
after the wedding day.

Nell continued to work in the greengrocer's on
Aigburth Road. Jack painted houses for his Brother-In-
Law, Tom Powell, who had started a painting and
decorating business.

Tom Powell ran his very successful decorating
business for over thirty years. Tom wallpapered and
painted people's rooms around the area. He was very
skilled in his trade, and so he became quite a legend.
Most of his business came from referrals. Tom could
paint the exterior of a huge building or wallpaper a
little bathroom. He took all the jobs in stride. When
Tom Powell signed up for the Army in 1939, he placed
his business on the back burner. Each time Tom
returned home on a leave, he would work a few quick
jobs. Tom often helped out neighbours by redoing a

room for nothing more than a cup of tea. He had a heart of gold and was especially kind and giving to his elderly neighbours who could not afford to have their places painted or redecorated.

Chapter Seven

The King's Speech

The summer of 1939 was a very scary time for Liverpudlians. The *Echo* was full of war talk. Lucy or Eileen would read out the latest stories from the war and how close it was coming. Sheer panic crept in as each day featured more frightening headlines.

Gladys Whitney looked down to her new baby Jeanie in her crib and choked back tears. With two little kids and Tom Whitney still away at sea, she felt trepidation. Tom was gone most of the time, and war with Germany made the oceans so dangerous that she feared she would never see him again.

As the whole of England tuned their radios in on that Friday night, 3rd September 1939, ready to hear the King's speech, the family gathered round at Lucy's Mum's house. The fire roared behind them, but some of the women shivered awaiting the news. The room filled with thick smoke, as the adults puffed their brains out.

"In this grave hour," said King George, "perhaps the most fateful in history, I send to every household of my peoples, both at home and overseas, this message spoken with the same depth of feeling for each one of you as if I were able to cross your threshold and speak to you myself. For the second time this century, we are at war."

Everyone gasped.

"Over and over again," said the King, "we have tried to find a peaceful way out of the differences between ourselves and those who are now our enemies, but it has been in vain. We have been forced into a conflict for which we are called with our allies to meet the challenge of a principle, which, if it were to prevail, would be fatal to any civilized order in the world. It is a principle which permits a state in the selfish pursuit of power to disregard its treaties and its solemn pledges, which sanctions the use of force or threat of force against the sovereignty and independence of other states. Such a principle stripped of all disguise, is surely the mere primitive doctrine that might is right, and if this principle were established throughout the world, the freedom of our own country and the whole British commonwealth of nations would be in danger. But far more than this, the peoples of the world would be kept in bondage of fear, and all hopes of settled peace and security of justice and liberty among nations would be ended. This is the ultimate issue which confronts us. For the sake of we ourselves hold dear, and of the world order and peace, it is unthinkable that we should refuse to meet the challenge. It is to this high purpose that I now call my people at home and my people across the seas who will make our cause their own. I ask them to stand calm and firm and united in this time of trial. The task will be hard. There may be dark days ahead, and war can no longer be confined to the battlefield, but we can only do the right as we see the right, and reverently commit our cause to God. If one and all we keep resolutely faithful to it, ready for whatever service or sacrifice it may demand, then with God's help we shall prevail. May He bless us and keep us all."

As King George's ominous speech finished everyone clung onto each other sobbing. Jack Whitney sat quietly in the corner, punching his fist into his left hand. It was his sixteenth birthday, but this was no time for celebrations.

Lucy's Dad broke the silence. "Go run up and get the *Echo*, Jack. I 'avn't even read it today."

Jack rushed off to the newspaper shop, where it was mobbed. The headline across the top read, *Germany Marches on Poland.*

A neighbour shouted out, "It's those German bastards started this!"

Another customer replied, "Bleedin' terrible. Someone has to stop them or they'll be marchin' on us next."

"Yer right," answered Jack. "We 'ave to stop

'em." He brought the copy of the *Echo* home, and then ran up the street to the corner pub to order his first pint. Jack sat in there drinking all night, the beer building up his courage as he planned his next move. Jack knew exactly what he wanted to do, first thing Monday.

He woke up, dressed and left without breakfast, just a quick swig of hot tea. Instead of heading into work to paint Mary Brown's front parlour, Jack marched downtown to the Liverpool recruitment office.

After a few hours he was all signed up. Jack used Tom's birth certificate, eleven years his senior, to enlist in the Merchant Navy. Walking back, he sported a new naval uniform. He was bedazzled at the prospect of shipping out and heading off to war.

Jack didn't realize that the recruitment office didn't care which ID you produced as long as you were willing to go off and fight. Many young lads signed up using their big brother's or uncle's ID. Lads as young as fourteen enlisted by the thousands.

Jack Whitney rode the tram back to Lark Lane and charged down Bickerton Street with his head held high.

His tiny five-foot Mam, with her Irish brogue, nearly had a heart attack.

"Sweet mother of Jesus! What are ye doing, lad?"

"I'm shippin' out tomorrow," Jack announced, shoulders back and head high, as his Mum slumped down into her chair.

"Oh dear God. You're just a lad. You're far too young to go fight, son."

"No I'm not," Jack said. "Tommy O'Hara joined as well. He just turned sixteen like me." Tommy had been Jack's best friend since they were infants.

"Can I not talk you out of it?"

"Nah. Mam. I 'ave to go. I want to fight those Germans."

His Dad sat there silently throughout the conversation. He stood up and put his arms around Jack. "I'm proud of yer, lad. But you know we'll be worried."

Although she felt weak with nerves, Jack's Mam cooked up his favorite dinner: lamb chops and roasties. She choked down her meal that night.

Jack's sister Nell sat at the table sobbing. Jack told her not to worry and enveloped her in a warm hug before going out for a couple of drinks at the Albert. His friends toasted his departure.

Early the next morning, Tommy O'Hara knocked at the door, his eyes sparkly with excitement. He looked young and handsome in his naval uniform, and was going to be trained as a gunner with Jack on the armed merchant navy vessels.

"Are ye ready to go bury a Jerry?" he asked.

"As ready as I'll ever be."

Jack's Mam stood at the door, wiping her eyes.

"Don't cry, Mam," said Jack. "I'll send yer letters." With that, he kissed her on the forehead and left.

His Mam's knees buckled, and she watched her youngest lad charge up the street eager to go fight for his country. "Please watch over him, he is just a lad," she asked God as she sobbed her heart out.

The *Harmodius* was a steam-powered merchant ship of over 5,000 tons. The vessel, armed with machine guns and artillery, towered above the two young boys.

Jack Whitney arrived at the port side. "Isn't she great, Tommy?"

"She certainly is. I can't wait to sail."

The news of Jack's enlisting spread through the family. Gladys wrote a letter to Tom to let him know his kid brother had signed up. Tom wrote to Jack, and they were able to keep in touch weekly throughout the war.

Six months training for new recruits, Jack was stationed down in London first. There he met a girl named Joyce. Joyce was about five-feet four-inches, with lovely blonde hair and gorgeous complexion. I can remember her helping us as little kids with a variety of jobs we were assigned, from peeling spuds to helping with our homework assignments.

Uncle Jack often entered ballroom dancing competitions. He and Joyce were great dancers. Despite the war, they had fun nights out.

But, soon enough, everything changed when the war finally arrived in Liverpool and London in the form of German bombers filling the skies and dropping their payloads in the night.

Just days before Prime Minister Chamberlain made his official war declaration over the radio, the Liverpool Corporation began to evacuate children to Cheshire and North Wales. The countryside was much safer from bomb attacks than the vital port city that was Liverpool. The Germans would surely target the ports and ships.

For many parents, this was the only way available to ensure their children would survive, even if Britain fell to Hitler.

After war was officially declared, months passed by unexpectedly. The bombs didn't arrive right away. This was called a "phony war," and many of the children returned to Liverpool.

However, once France collapsed to the Nazis in May of 1940, the German Luftwaffe moved right to the edge of the English Channel. That's when the Blitz began in earnest.

Kids reacted in many different ways to the upheaval. Some were frightened. Others saw it as a great adventure. Many had never been to the countryside, nor seen fields or farm animals, and they were overwhelmed by their new surroundings.

Once children arrived at their country destinations with gas masks slung across their shoulders, they were selected by billeters, who often made decisions based on appearances. The strong, healthy kids were separated from their weaker or smaller siblings, which was traumatic for them.

Some children were not chosen at all, and they were transferred from home to home by the organizers. Many billeters were shocked by the states of the poor inner-city children. Kids arrived filthy and in tatters, with lice, malnutrition, and diseases. Impetigo, scabies, and diphtheria were common in

densely populated urban areas but not in the
countryside.

Many of the kids had wonderful times. Some
even refused to leave at the end of the war. They opted
to stay with their host families and a better life. Some
chose to be adopted by their billeted parents.

Mothers suffered terribly, missing their
children and coping with bomb raids, rationing, and
the absence and even deaths of their husbands. They
were asked to pay what they could afford toward their
children's upkeep.

Parents were permitted to visit but were
encouraged not to do so. Often this unsettled the
children. Consequently, mothers knew little about the
people who were raising their kids.

No doubt the evacuation of children from
Britain's cities during the Blitz saved numerous lives.
Approximately 130,000 people were evacuated from
Merseyside. Children were sent from all the large cities
that were vulnerable to air raids. Not only
schoolchildren but also pregnant women, young

mothers with babies, and disabled adults fled from the bombs.

Some local children had been sent off to Wales, but my Mum insisted she would be fine with us still in Liverpool. We had air raid shelters on our street, so that made her feel safer. It took tremendous courage for the Mums to send their kids away.

All the Mums in our family kept their children with them.

My Aunty Eileen left Liverpool in May, after one of the nightly air raids. She took her two small children, my cousins Eileen and Fred, and travelled by train to East Grinstead. This was close to the base my Uncle Tom Powell was stationed at.

Even today, 78 years later, my cousin Eileen recalls fond memories of the wonderful nine months they spent there with a family who shared their hearts and home with them.

So many gladly took in city families who fled the bombing raids.

Chapter Eight

The First Bombs

On the night that the German planes first headed for Liverpool, Herby Doyle told Lucy to hide under the stairs. He didn't think the shelters were so safe. A shelter had recently been bombed. She was pregnant with her first baby and struggling to cope with morning sickness.

Lucy stuck a pillow under the staircase to lie on. Then she snuggled up and covered herself with a comforter. She was shaking with fear as the German bombs began to explode at the docks.

Hundreds of bombs exploded across the port, seeking to put Liverpool out of commission. My Mum said she could taste the residue from the bombs. It lingered around in the air for days.

My Dad, Herby, was the only husband in the family still in Liverpool. At the time of the first air raid, he was out on Home Guard fire watch at the Dingle. On some nights he was posted at Edge Lane.

German bombers came relentlessly night after night. Liverpool was a major shipping center. Her docks were prime targets for the Jerries.

A particularly large air raid shelter was the *Ernest Brown Junior Instructional Centre* on Durning Road in Edge Hill. A reinforced ceiling offered protection to the public in the basement and boiler room.

On the evening of 28th November, 1940, the warning sirens screamed out. Local residents raced over to the *Ernest Brown* shelter. Men, women and children dressed warmly, and mothers wrapped their babies up in blankets.

Shops had been flattened all around. The crowd climbed over rubble to get to the shelter door. People became desperate as the bombs got closer. More than three-hundred people entered the basement as the bombs began to fall across the city.

The Abbots were a close knit family from the Dingle area. Their father, Tom Abbot, a handsome blonde-headed man over six-feet tall was disabled due to childhood polio, and he used crutches. His daughters ran toward the *Ernest Brown Centre* with their Mum, Mary.

My Aunty Nell's Mother-In-Law had gone to school with Mary Abbott. She was a dear friend. Ellen was ten-years-old, and Betsy was seven. Baby Catherine was only eight months.

At the outer door, Mary panicked. "Oh God, Tom, I've forgotten the baby's bag." They paused at the entrance, as the crowd poured inside.

"Go on, love," Tom said. "Get the kids in before the first bombs. I'll get back home and pass it in later."

"Oh, Tom, love, please be careful." Mary grabbed him for a kiss. She and the children slipped inside just before the doors were sealed.

Mary had no nappies for her little girl and no bottles to see her through the night. Their house wasn't too far away. So Tom made it there and back pretty quickly.

As Tom Abbot returned to the shelter with the baby's bag, he saw a parachute bomb drop onto the massive building.

At 1:55am, the school took a direct hit from a parachute mine. The entire building collapsed, sending debris straight onto those sheltered in the basement. Many people were buried alive.

The boiler burst, streaming out hot water, and shattered gas pipes ignited. Anyone not killed outright faced steam and fires inside the collapsed structure. Above them, what was left of the building was ablaze. Rescue workers struggled to free survivors.

During the next two days, the rescue effort went on. First the survivors, and then the bodies of the dead were hauled to the surface. Trying to retrieve all the casualties was hopeless, and the call was made to cover the area in lime and seal it over.

Police figures gave the total number of dead as one hundred and sixty six. However, it was widely believed that the number was larger at around one hundred and eighty.

Of the survivors, only thirty people were rescued unharmed. Many spoke of having to walk over the bodies of the dead to escape. Many of the victims remained unidentified, and they were all buried together in a grave at the Anfield Cemetery.

Tom Abbott collapsed to the ground, knowing that his wife and daughters would not have survived. He lived out his days as a broken man.

My Aunty Eileen told this story many times. Apparently, Mary Abbott was her neighbour's best friend from school.

Chapter Nine

Lucy Has Her First Baby

L ucy Doyle brought out her little suitcase and packed a few belongings, as stabbing labour pains shot down her back. Her Mum accompanied her to Oxford Street Hospital. This hospital had a nice maternity section, a long ward with beds on each side. The delivery room sat right off the ward. There were no phones by the beds and no TV. So, the Mums spent their days helping one another with tips on how to cope in their new roles as mothers.

After seven hours in labour, Lucy delivered her first baby, a little girl. She named her Jean. It was 1941 and Lucy now had a brand new baby to worry about in addition to her own survival. War news was on the radio at all hours. It was a very scary time, for the new

Mums in the family.

Lucy with baby Jean | credit: Doreen Doyle

Lucy felt overjoyed with he r new baby girl. She visited her sister Eileen and her Sister-In-Law, Gladys. There was a break in the nightly bombings, and Liverpool life had returned to a kind of normalcy.

For the first few weeks of her life, it was nice and calm for Lucy and her new baby. Baby Jean was six-weeks old when the May Blitz attacked Liverpool.

Chapter Ten

The May Blitz of 1941

L uftwaffe bombers appeared over the city every single night. As the Doyles lived nearby the docks, Herby gave Lucy meticulous instructions to stay safe inside. But the bombs fell closer to their house every night. Lucy cowered under the staircase, petrified, clutching her helpless little baby girl. Herby told Mum not to wait until the planes were close, and to take supplies, nappies and any items needed for Jean. Lucy pushed her pillow and comforter as deep under the stairs as possible. She lay there terrified, listening for the warplanes to cross over her house.

During one air raid, a bomb screeched down onto the roof above. She squeezed beneath the stairs just as the bomb struck the house. The blast blew it completely off the house.

With a massive whoosh, all the soot from the chimney filled her front parlor, covering over her clean baby clothes and nappies on the maiden in front of the fireplace.

When the war later quieted down, Lucy climbed back out from under the stairs and assessed the damage. After her initial shock wore off, she declared, "Oh, sweet mother of Jesus. Me new nappies all ruined after me boiling the shite out of them."

Herby was out on fire watch a few miles away, where he saw the bombs fall close to their street. On his bicycle, he frantically raced back home while more bombs continued to drop. His heart thumping in his chest, he stood up on the pedals and sprinted home as fast as he could.

As Herby arrived at the house, another blast threw him to the ground. He rolled over and looked up to see his neighbor, Harry Ashcroft, blown to bits against his own front door.

Hurrying in, Herby shouted for Lucy. She and the baby had hidden again and clung to each other in the mangled staircase. As they all escaped the damaged structure, Herby shielded Lucy and little Jean from the sight of their dead next-door neighbor.

The air was thick with the stench of war, bombs, and death. Police and ambulance sirens screamed throughout the city. The blasts were deafening. People searched for loved ones, digging through the rubble of their flattened houses with bare hands and calling out the names of loved ones.

"Mary, Danny, Millie can you hear me?" One lady sobbed as she cleared debris, hoping her family was still alive under the rubble.

Herby and Lucy passed by some bodies covered in white sheets streaked with debris and blood.

More bombs. Terror crackled in Lucy's voice, "Oh God, Herb! They're dropping near our Tom's house."

"I'll check on them as soon as I can get you someplace safe," he said.

They heard more planes flying overhead.

Two neighbour women held hands and prayed together, trembling with fear as the barrage of bombs again rained down around them.

There were no air raid shelters on Wellington Road. Herby did not want to take a chance on finding one close by. Most would be filled to capacity. I t was just as dangerous to try and find a new place. Nowhere was safe. So they went to the neighbour's house to borrow a handcart and feed baby Jean.

The bombing paused and Herby returned with the borrowed handcart piled with their belongings, He had tied their thin mattress around the cart with string.

"Let's get you down to me Mum's in Aigburth," Herby said. "It's safer down there away from the docks."

They walked down Park Road and climbed over bricks from the bombed places,shops that had been completely demolished. Houses burned. They passed more dead bodies waiting for the morgue to pick them up.

Herby encouraged Mum. "Be brave love. We're going to get through this. I promise."

Lucy sobbed as she pushed the pram full of her meager possessions, holding onto baby Jean with all her might. The family reached Aigburth Road which had not been bombed. The side was clear for them to push the mattress and handcart and the pram full of their most valuable possessions.

There were a few nice dishes and a set of brass candlesticks, which I still have today. My Aunty Jean, a rosy cheeked Aunty with brown eyes and light brown hair, had given them for a wedding gift. Aunty Jean was my Dad's sister and a huge part of my parents lives back then. They spent many hours at her house, when her children were small. Mum and Dad also had a small mirror for above the fireplace, nothing of much value except to them.

Mum and Dad continued their trek to the Vale, cutting up Lark Lane and through Sefton Park. It was a good six miles. As they struggled with their belongings more German planes flew past overhead toward the ports. They heard many bombs fall and explode back where they had escaped from.

The pair paused briefly in Sefton Park, where it felt like a different world. It was so calm and peaceful away from the war.

Herby's Mum knew about a house for rent further up her street. Lots of houses remained vacant after the exodus to the countryside. Hers was number 23 on Briarwood Road. The house for rent on Briarwood was number 53.

Herby and Lucy shuffled back and forth to move all their furnishings out to safer ground. After five or six days of back and forth trips, they managed to piece together a livable home on Briarwood Road for seven shillings a week.

Lucy Doyle would give birth to four children in that little two-up/two-down house with no running hot water and no inside toilet. Our lavatory was down in the backyard. We would take chambers upstairs each night to wee in and then had the job of emptying them out and scrubbing them each morning.

Life on Briarwood Road was very hard on my Mum. To bathe us, she had to struggle in with a five-foot steel bathtub, which was hung on the backyard wall. Next, she boiled kettles and the few pans she had on the stove. After a good hour or so we would have several inches of hot water in the tub. She set it in front of the fire, and this was our Saturday night routine.

I hated when my bare back touched the icy steel sides of the tub. Scrubbed down with a bar of *Fairy Soap*, we never had any shampoo until we grew up and bought our own.

On Saturdays, each kid took turns scrubbing the wooden seat of the lavatory, and then the toilet and floor. Our toilet paper was the *Liverpool Echo* cut into eight-inch squares. With a nail through the center, these were hung on a string from the pipes by the tank. We filled three strings a week. That would do us all to wipe our bums.

Our only entertainment was the free library on

Aigburth Road. We all went each week and were avid readers. My Mum filled the deep part of the baby's pram with books. We read all the children's classics, *Robinson Crusoe, Little Women, Gulliver's Travels* etc. Lucy and Herby shared their books. So they both read four books a week.

We often sat in the library for a few hours if the baby was asleep in the pram. It was nice and quiet to begin our books for the week, also lovely and warm, with electric lights. The library had long shiny oak tables, with benches on each side, two of them in the children's section. The librarian would allow Mum to bring in the pram if the baby was asleep.

Our house was only warm in the kitchen, and the only lights were little candles placed all around in saucers of water. We couldn't wait to read at night, but we had no electricity money yet.

When we ran out of books, my Dad would make up stories of birds and rabbits. He'd go on until the little bird or rabbit in the story turned sleepy and wanted to go to bed. He kept talking as we trudged up the stairs and off to slumber. These were the happiest times of my life.

Lucy got together with Aunty Eileen at least twice a week. They brought along butties and a flask of tea and met up at the cafe in the park for a nice afternoon. Their weekly routine helped keep everyone informed on the current family developments. Sometimes Nell joined them, sometimes Gladys with her children. Especially during the summer months, it was a great way to stay informed. Of course, much was happening with the world at war.

Chapter Eleven

Glady's Street Bombed

More than 160 Planes bombed Liverpool that night, almost destroying St. Luke's Church on the top of Bold Street. My Grandad saw the devastation firsthand on his way home from work. The church was still burning. It became known as the bombed-out church. St. Luke's was an Anglican Parish church built in the 1800s and was used as a concert hall.

Herby called around to Woodruff Street to see if Gladys and the kids were okay, but he was shocked to see her house completely demolished.

"Oh dear God." He searched for them.

It was absolute chaos on the street, with houses destroyed on each side. Home Guards covered the dead bodies and arranged for ambulances and hearses. Badly injured people lay out on blankets waiting for the ambulances to arrive.

Peter and Jeanie, May 1941, the rubble of 37 Woodruff Street | credit: Peter Whitney

Wonderful, caring neighbours provided meals somehow to help the wounded make it through the night. No one had much to spare, but everyone pitched in.

People would say, "This is the best soup I've ever tasted."

Sometimes it was a nice vegetable soup or a brown gravy stew. It felt such a relief to have such caring neighbours, as the poor souls watched their homes burn down.

Tom Whitney was away at sea, and Gladys had been left in her house with her three little ones, including her six-week-old baby girl, little Gladys.

Herby could find no trace of them in the chaos and smoke.

Mr. Boardman, a close neighbour, came over to Herby and introduced himself. He said, "She's at the *Florence Institute* lad, got hit in the head with flying glass. The kids are okay though." Mr. Boardman was a tall, silver-haired man in his early 60s with rosy cheeks. Luckily his own house hadn't been bombed.

Mr. Boardman told Herby that Gladys would move into number 32 across the street.

Herby began to save some clothes, pots and

pans, anything he could salvage. Mr. Boardman helped him dig out the beds. The two men worked for several hours trying to save Gladys' belongings.

Once they moved the stuff out of the rubble, Herby went to find Gladys and the kids at the *Florence Institute*. The space was crammed full of casualties with arms and legs hanging off of stretchers, children with holes in their legs and terribly gruesome injuries everywhere.

"Oh dear God," Herby mumbled. "Poor bugger."

One lady was severely burned. About 100 people waited in triage just to be treated.

Herby Doyle located Gladys, all bandaged up, with a turban wrapped around her head, her face was still black with soot.

"Oh Herb,"she said and relayed the story to him. "I thought we were all done for. I hear the bomb coming. I put me hand over our Gladys face. Next thing you know I'm hit in the head with a massive piece of glass, cut it wide open. Our little Peter was scared stiff."

Her blood had dripped all over her yellow and blue dress.

"He was a proper good lad getting me a towel to wrap around me head. Wern't ye, lad?"

Five-year-old Peter was beaming.

Gladys and my two cousins at the new house | credit: Peter Whitney

Gladys said, "I suddenly realized our Jeannie was in the front room. Go see if she's okay lad. I told our Peter. He had to climb over the mess to see her. And the little bugger said, 'I'm not scared of that Bastard Hitler.' Kids, they make you laugh hey Herb?"

The two burst out laughing.

Gladys relaxed on hergurney. "The watchman shouted, 'All dead in 37,' and I shouted back, 'were in here mate!' So they dug us out."

Herby threw his arms around them. "I'm so glad you're all alright. We'll get through this. Just keep your chins up!"

Herby gave Gladys a long hug.

Peter exclaimed, "Hey Uncle Herby, I'm picking up all the pieces of shrapnel and bombs I can find. Me mates are having a competition o n who finds the best stuff."

"What a smashing idea," said Herby. "Good for you, lad."

"Look what I found on Woodruff Street yesterday!" Peter pulled out something from his bag.

"Wowzer," said Herby. "That is a beauty."

Peter showed off an incendiary bomb not yet

exploded with a circular plate around a fin and frayed edges.

"Me Mam said I can put it on the fireplace to show everyone."

"Smashing that, lad," said Herby. "Take care of yer Mam. I'll stop over again."

Gladys shouted, "Tara Herb."

"Tara Uncle Herb," the kids shouted.

Off Herby returned to his Fire Watch shift in the Home Guard.

Peter returned to his bombed-out house to find some nappies for his baby sister and towels. He saw some buried in the rubble.

"Oh me Mam will be made up." He piled as many as he could carry on his outstretched arms.

He did hear a plane above.

"Oh God," he said out loud as the plane targeted the people on the street and dropped a bomb.

Little Peter was thrown far from the blast. Some of the nappies and towels were blown to bits. He lay face down on the street for minutes before the night watchman, Mr. O'Leary, found him lying there.

"Phone an ambulance!" He shouted and blew his whistle.

Mr. McGreggor, the pub manager, ran back to his pub on the corner to make the phone call.

The ambulance arrived in 15 minutes, and they lifted Peter onto a stretcher. Gladys came running across the street with Jeanie and baby Gladys.

"I'll 'ave to go with him," she said. "Ees just a little lad."

The ambulance driver agreed. "We can't take all the kids though."

Mrs. Boardman stepped in. "Ere, Glad you pass them to me," she said. "You just worry about Peter."

Gladys' terrific neighbour, she often referred to Mrs. Boardman as "an absolute Godsend."

Off they drove to Smithdown Road Hospital, where little Tommy had died years before. Peter was placed in a kaolin poultice, similar to ones used on broken bones. His intestines had all shifted upwards from the force of the shockwave.

Twelve people were killed down the street from Gladys' house. Houses all around hers were flattened under the deluge of German bombs: eight on Woodruff Street, with six on their side of the street and two across, plus five on Harlow and seven on Wellington Road, Lucy's street. Lucy's next-door neighbour and six houses on Denton street had also been flattened.

No matter how bad it got during the Blitz, people scampered to the shops to retrieve food in the daytime. Often meeting neighbours who had lost everything, like Gladys Whitney, sheer inner strength kept these brave women going against all odds.

Peter, who is now in his 80s, recently visited a World War Two exhibit with his family. An old film started, and the sounds of the bombs dropping came alive. He began to tremble and couldn't stop a complete panic attack. All those memories of that little lad getting nappies for his Mum came flooding back. He remembered almost being killed, and he had to leave the exhibit.

Little Peter was stuck at Smithdown Hospital in Intensive Care for four weeks.

Chapter Twelve

"Jarmony" Calling

Besides being obsessed with the lack of food, everyone in the neighborhood fixated on the nightly rantings of Lord Haw Haw and his distinct upper-class accent. He worked for the Third Reich taunting the population of England with rambling propaganda. This was psychological warfare.

"Jarmony calling," he started each broadcast.

Gladys Whitney listened in one Saturday night during the Battle of the Atlantic, desperate for any news that might help her find out if Tom and his brother Jack were safe.

Lord Haw Haw announced over the wireless, "You have lost. Your sons are all dying! Our superior navy has just sunk the *Harmodius*. No survivors. Your sons are dead. Give up. You cannot beat us. Our superior navy is winning."

Gladys slumped down into a heap. She knew that was Jack Whitney's ship. She piled her kids onto the pram so she could run around to her Mother-In-Law's house. When she arrived, Lucy and Nell sat sobbing, holding onto each other. Jack's little Mum lay on her sofa crying her heart out.

Eileen arrived next, breathless with Fred and little Eileen. "Don't believe it, Mam," she said. "He tells lies. Let's wait and see what the BBC says about survivors."

They waited tensely for the 8 O'clock news to start. When it did, the first announcement was the sinking of the *Harmodius*. The news anchor tried to reassure the listeners. "We are trying to determine if there are any survivors. The battle is still going on, so difficult to get an assessment. Don't give up hope."

Eileen asked, "What do yer think, Mam?"

"Oh, maybe some men will survive," said her

Mum. "Please God let me lad be one of 'em."

The Battle of the Atlantic raged for months. More than 3,000 ships were sunk, and so many lives were lost. Every night Lord Haw Haw gloated on the events of the previous day, trying to dishearten the British public.

Some ships were disabled and scuttled. Survivors floated in the freezing north Atlantic waters while the battle continued.

As the Whitney family fretted, out on the Atlantic, Captain DeSalis, of the HMS *Faulknor*, announced over the ship's loudspeakers, "We have spotted some men in the water. We are proceeding towards them now."

Tom Whitney was on the top deck of the HMS *Faulknor*. "God!" he shouted, "I'm not a religious man, but please let one of these be our Jack."

Tom ran down the decks overcome with emotion and sobbing. His heart pounded in his chest as they started pulling survivors out of the water. He kept repeating "Please God, he's just a lad."

They hooked the men and pulled them up on board the *Faulknor* like sacks of potatoes. The wretches were coated over in black oil and half frozen to death.

Tom Whitney sprinted over to each survivor and gazed down into their oily faces. Out of the thirty sailors taken from the water, he made it to number twenty-three and screamed out, "Jack!"

Tom grabbed hold of his kid brother's hand, which was weak and limp.

"Our kid is alive!" he called to the crew who knew about his plight. "Alright are yer, lad?"

"I've been better," Jack replied through chattering teeth, "Bleeding hell, Tom. Me legs are frozen!"

The two Scouser brothers sobbed with relief, happy to be alive. The odds were against them finding each other in the middle of the war for the Atlantic.

"Yerl be alright now lad. Mam and Dad will be over the moon," Tom whispered to his half-dead kid brother.

The battle continued around them.

Jack, who was eighteen, suffered from hypothermia and fatigue. He was quickly taken into the ship's hospital. The surviving men were cleaned off and fed. Jack spent the next two weeks in sick bay. He was then transferred to the HMS *Forrester*.

Jack Whitney seldom spoke about the war for the rest of his life. Tom, on the other hand, told the family all the war stories and the actions of his ships.

Both Whitney brothers met up again in Alexandria. Jack finally opened up to his big brother about his time in the icy waters. Tom wrote home and told his Mam all about it.

Tommy O'Hara, Jack's school friend, escaped from the sinking *Harmodius* with him. The two boys floated together side by side for many hours, while U-boat torpedoes exploded all around them.

Tommy steadily lost his mind. "I can't take no more!" he said. The waves crashed over them relentlessly.

"Don't give up, mate." Jack begged Tommy to

hang on, as hours passed and the battle continued relentlessly.

Some of the surviving men prayed. Some shouted, "Are you listening, God? We just want to get home."

As their body temperatures dropped and they increasingly froze, some of the lads sang songs. *Rule Britannia* and *Land of Hope and Glory* were preferred.

Some shouted jokes to each other as they bobbed in the freezing water. "Our soldiers went to war. Our soldiers won. Our soldiers stuck their bayonets up the German's our soldiers went to war..."

When a German ship or plane was hit by fire, they all cheered in unison.

After six hours of bombs and icy seawater, Tommy couldn't take any more. He pulled the plug on his life vest and drowned.

Jack never recovered from losing his best mate that way.

The *Harmodius* was transporting pig iron and other cargo bound for Glasgow, Scotland. My Uncle's ship was one of hundreds sunk in March and April of that year. The pain and joy our family felt has lasted over seventy years. We were so relieved to know Uncle Jack lived through that terrible ordeal.

When my Uncle Jack came down to Liverpool to visit, they would tell his story to the men in the local pub. Everyone sent a drink over. "Toast them men. God bless them both," they would declare. Most of the time the two would end up plastered.

Tom Whitney sent his wife Gladys letters from the war whenever he could, with photos of the various battles he was part of. Sometimes Gladys received correspondence from the Navy stating Tom owed them money. He had been fined for fighting or getting drunk. Gladys had to try to feed her kids until the next money came.

So poor, she would use an *Oxo*, a dried cube of beef stock, with enough water to fill a cup each. They would dunk in bread. The dog shared the same dinner, *Oxo* broth with bread. Occasionally, Gladys and Lucy had to scrub the peelings thrown out from the day

before and fashion some kind of soup from them.
Fried bread in bacon grease was a regular item for tea,
but the kids survived regardless of their poor
nutrition.

Gladys would get livid with Tom for leaving
them in such a desperate position, but she knew it was
because of the war and all he was going through at the
time.

The Salvation Army gave out free soup every
Thursday at the Dingle. Sometimes it was vegetable
soup. The smell was wonderful to hungry kids waiting
in line with bowls. Once the word spread, the queues
grew so long that it literally took hours to get your
bowl of soup.

Times were grueling. No one had much, but no
one ever starved. Neighbors always helped out with a
few potatoes or a couple of *Oxos* to keep the little ones
fed.

Most of the local Mums had to pawn anything
of value to feed their children after the money ran out.
My Mum would often go without her thin wedding

ring for months before she could buy it back again.

Today, I wear it on a chain around my neck as a reminder of how wonderful she was.

When the war finally ended, a young soldier named Geoffrey Perry was serving in the British Royal Pioneer Corps, assigned to T Force. Along with his Captain, Bertie Lickorish, they were enforcing the Allied military occupation of defeated Germany. Near the house they were occupying, the two spotted a suspicious character dash off into the woods. They chased him down.

The man reached into his pocket, and Geoffrey Perry immediately shot him in his bum, believing he was reaching for a gun.

The bleeding man presented an ID. Geoffrey was now afraid he would be court-martialed for shooting an unarmed German civilian. A few minutes later Captain Lickorish dug out a second set of IDs from the man's pocket, identifying him as William James Bray, the infamous Lord Haw Haw.

James Bray was tried for Treason and hung

in1946.

Chapter Thirteen

The German Pilot

It was 1941, and the Blitz was devastating Liverpool each night. German planes filled the skies as bombs fell and fires erupted across the city. As Herby Doyle came around the corner on his bicycle, he heard bombs exploding on Durnham Road.

"Jesus I think that's the Training College," he said to himself. He then heard a sound he had never heard before, like aloud whistling. He looked up and saw a plane on fire descending toward Durning Road.

"Christ. It's a crash." The burning aircraft hit the ground with tremendous force spewing flames.

Herby raced ahead to the site. There he saw two men in the plane, a pilot and an observer. He used his bayonet to cut the straps holding in the young pilot.

He was a German, about 23 years old, with a gaping hole in his stomach bleeding profusely.

The observer wasn't badly hurt.

A crowd of local residents formed at the crash site, and one man grabbed the two chains on the observer's neck, a crucifix and a swastika.

"Let's hang the swines." People in the crowd began to shout.

Herby put his arms up in the air, "Hold on," he said. "I need to get this young lad to the First Aid."

No one would help him and instead taunted him for wanting to help the enemy. Bombs were still falling all around the city.

Herby left another Home Guard mate to watch the two German airmen and ran off to the closest pub.

Entering, he announced, "I need some help. I have a young lad bleeding all over the place. The pub crowd stared solemnly back at him.

Tommy Jones called back, "Yah want us to 'elp you with the bastards who just bombed the training college?"

"Yeah," said Herby. "Our lads are over there bombing the shite out of their houses. Would you want one of them to bleed to death cos no one would help?"

The pub men thought it over for a minute.

"Come on, lads. Give me a hand." Herby asked again.

Freddy Roberts and Tommy Jones swilled down their pints and followed Herby out to where the two Germans had crashed.

The pilot rambled on, "Mein Gott" (My God). He was doubled up in agony with the stomach wound.

Tommy asked Herby, "Whats he saying?"

"Dunno. Something about he's got."

Freddy leaned over him and said, "What ya got Jerry is a dirty big ole in ya belly. Shut ya gob and we'll take ya the First Aid."

The pilot nodded. They carried him up Durning Road to the closest police station that had a First Aid section, in Edge Hill. The nurse in charge, Connie Ashcroft, warned the pilot,"Yer better behave yerself."

The German was half dead and not much of a threat.

They carried him past her as she complained, "Yer lucky we ave good hearts here, lad!" Nurse Ashcroft bandaged a young boy's head, who had just been gashed in the raid.

Herby lifted up the pilot onto a gurney and said, "Ya will be alright now, lad."

The weeping German grabbed my Dads hand and said, "Danke (Thank you)." They crashed Luftwaffe men were later transferred to the hospital and they both survived thanks to my Dad. Herby was very proud to tell this story throughout his life, how he did not lose his humanity at the worst time in Liverpool's history.

Chapter Fourteen

The Battle of The Atlantic

*"The only thing that ever really frightened
me during the war was the U-Boat peril."*
-Winston Churchill

The Battle of the Atlantic, which lasted from
September 1939 until the defeat of Germany
in 1945, was the war's longest continuous
military campaign. During six years of naval warfare,
German U-Boats and warships, and later Italian
submarines, were pitted against allied convoys
transporting military equipment and supplies across
the Atlantic Ocean to Great Britain and the Soviet
Union. This sea war to control the Atlantic's shipping
lanes consisted of thousands of ships stretched across

thousands of perilous square miles of ocean.

German warships made a number of forays into the shipping lanes early in the war. These had limited success and led to the loss of major ships including *Graf-Spee* and the *Bismarck*. From 1940 onward, the German Navy focused on using U-Boats for stealth attacks. Attacking on the surface at night, they couldn't be detected by allied sonar (ASDIC).

U-Boats devastated the allied convoys, and they sank numerous merchant ships with torpedoes. The U-Boats could quickly submerge and evade the counter attacks by the escorting allied warships. They also benefited from the decoded communications of the British Admiralty.

In 1941, German U-Boats inflicted huge losses and sank over 800 allied ships. After then, the tactical advantage began to shift towards the British.

The UK received 50 American destroyers in exchange for US access to British bases. Canada increased their escort missions too, and the RAF Coastal Command was able to increase its air cover.

But, the capture of U-110 including its "Enigma Machine" and codes, in March of 1941, is what provided the allies all the movements of the German U-Boats.

In April 1941, U.S. warships began escorting allied convoys as far as Iceland, sparking a number of skirmishes with U-Boats. This provoked controversy, as the U.S. had not officially entered the war yet.

Technological developments, including radar, which could detect U-Boat periscopes at a range of one mile, also worked in the allies' favor.

Yet, shipping convoys were still vulnerable in the "Atlantic Gap," a "black pit" in the middle of the Atlantic, which could not be covered by anti-submarine aircraft.

The gradual improvement of anti-submarine techniques, and the increased use of improvised aircraft carriers like HMS *Audacity*, led to a decrease in sinkings toward the end of the year.

All of these factors contributed to Hitler's decision, carried out against the German Admiral

Donitz's wishes, to transfer Germany's submarines down to the Mediterranean.

In 1942, the balance tilted again in favor of the Germans. New submarines entered service at a rate of twenty per month.

Although the U.S. Navy entered the war at the end of 1941, allied ship losses in the Atlantic reached their peak in 1942. After 1,664 ships were sunk, supplies of petrol and food to Britain reached critically low levels.

In 1943, the advantage shifted back to the allies again. With sufficient escort aircraft carriers and long-range aircraft to cover the Atlantic Gap, the battle reached its pinnacle between February and May of 1943.

The "Hedgehog" depth-charge mortar was one innovation that made life more dangerous for U-Boat crews. By *Black May*, 1943, U-Boat losses became unsustainable. One quarter of their fleet was sunk in one month.

Hitler withdrew his U-Boats from the Atlantic,

and the battle was won. Although new German submarines arrived in 1945, they came too late to affect the course of the war.

Historians estimated that more than 100 convoy battles took place during the Battle of the Atlantic. They cost the Merchant Navy more than 30,000 men and 3,000 ships. The equally terrible costs for the Germans was 783 U- Boats and 28,000 sailors lost.

When the news came over the BBC that Sunday, and they read the names of the men who had survived from the *Harmodius*, Jack's family cried with relief. Everyone at 19 Bickerton Street was overjoyed.

Nell was by now married to Tim O'Sullivan and pregnant with her first baby. Her Tim was away in the Royal Navy. So she lived with her Mum and Dad. She gave birth to a baby boy named Frank.

Nell's Dad still worked hard down in the Welsh coal mines. He already had developed "black lung" from the conditions there. They had very little money. Times were extraordinarily difficult for all.

Everything was rationed, but no one moaned or complained. They all just got on with it.

German bombing raids on Liverpool continued intermittently. Three nights of mass bombings at Christmas destroyed many of the streets of the city.

During the *May Blitz* of 1941 the bombs fell all night long. The time between May 1st and May 8th was the worst week of sustained bombing raids on any part of Britain. The Germans threw everything they had to try and wreck the port of Liverpool.

The city's center was obliterated. Huskisson Number Two Dock was destroyed when the *Malakand* was blown up. In Breckside, an ammunition train exploded and flattened the entire district.

The Liverpool Blitz was a sustained bombing of the entire area within the counties of Lancashire and Cheshire. Liverpool was the most heavily bombed area of the country outside of London, which was bombed for 57 consecutive nights beginning 7th September 1940.

Liverpool, along with Birkenhead, featured the

largest West Coast Port. It had the most strategic importance for the British war effort. The government concealed from the Germans just how much damage had been inflicted on the docks. Reports on the bombing were kept low-key. Around 4,000 people were killed in the Merseyside area during the Blitz. This death toll was second only to London, which suffered 30,000 deaths by the end of the war.

The port had for many years been the United Kingdom's main link with North America. This proved to be a key asset in Britain's participation in the Battle of the Atlantic. As well as providing anchorage for naval ships from many nations the Mersey Ports handled over 90 per cent of all the war material brought into Britain from abroad. Some 75 million tons passed through its 11 miles (18 km) of quays. Without this port, Britain could not have survived the war.

Chapter Fifteen

The Telegraph Pole

I t was bitterly cold at night during the winter of 1941. People on Briarwood Road burned old tires, shoes, anything they could find to try and keep warm.

Kids were often sent into Sefton Park during the days to drag home fallen branches. Families could afford to keep one little room heated. We spent most of our time in there, shivering in coats.

The German bombing raids came at night. So during the day everyone scampered to bring back milk, bread, and a bit of meat. Mums frantically cooked bits of food before they ran out of power. When the shilling ran out, the gas would cut off.

In the dark early morning hours, Herby Doyle came around Carnatic Drive on his bike on his way home from night watch at the Dingle. There he spotted a huge telegraph pole with all of its wires and lines disconnected.

He smiled and raced up Briarwood to his home.

"Where's me saw, love?" he called.

"Under the stairs, Herb," said Lucy.

"Come on! Get yer coat on. I've found a bleeding lifesaver!"

The baby was fast asleep. So they put her in her pram and ran down to the "bloom field" at the bottom of Briarwood Road, which is now an old people's home.

Herby started sawing through the huge telephone pole. He worked for hours. As the cut was almost entirely through, and the pole was rocking back and forth, a copper walked past.

"Quickly," Herby said, "pretend we're having a sweetheart moment. Grab the middle of the bleeding pole, love."

He and Lucy grabbed hold of one another—and the teetering telegraph pole—and started to kiss.

The policeman stopped in front of them.

"Time to go 'ome you two."

Lucy, my Mum | credit: Doreen Doyle

"Yeah, sorry," Herby said "Good night, officer."

They waited until he was well out of sight and

let go. *Whoosh!* The pole crashed down with such force

it destroyed the wooden fence of a huge field.

"Oh Jesus!" said Herby. "Quick, love, go and knock on the neighbors. Tell 'em come quick with saws. We 'ave enough firewood for the winter 'ere."

Lucy raced back to the street to spread the word. Soon the neighbors poured down the road with prams and saws and axes. The women worked all night long.

The neighbourhood Mums dragged huge wood chunks up the back entry of each house before the copper came back.

"Cover it all," said Herby. "They'll be around tomorrow looking fer it."

Sure enough, first thing Sunday morning, two detectives came up the street and knocked at each door with drag marks leading to their backyards.

The lead detective asked my Dad, "Seen anything of the telegraph pole that was cut down last night?"

"Nah," replied Herby. "We didn't hear a thing."

All the families gave the same story. The

detectives, being local lads, just accepted it and moved on. No follow-up was ever done.

But the people on Briarwood Road in Aigburth Vale talked about that night for the rest of their lives, how Herby Doyle had saved them all from freezing.

As a little girl, I was so proud when people praised my Dad for cutting down the telegraph pole and providing wood for all the neighbors. He was a local hero.

Once they found out we were Herby Doyle's kids, some of the shops gave us kids a biscuit or a sweet. I loved the pieces of fudge we occasionally received, so creamy I would eat it as slowly as possible it was such a treat.

Finally, in January 1942 the German bombers stopped their attack on Liverpool. People met up at the shops and held each other in massive hugs. They listened to the wild tales of death, destruction, and survival.

My Mum told everyone how her roof was blown off the house while she hid under the stairs, and how scared she had been, holding onto my big sister, who was only six-weeks old at that time.

Like most, Lucy struggled to find enough food, despite the fact that Herby never lost their money from fines. When we were given free lunches at school it was a huge relief. The schools gave children milk and free lunches provided by the Catholic charities.

Lucy cooked rice pudding every week, from the free dried milk which she got from the clinic on Lark Lane. It was intended for the baby, but used in this way the kids received extra nutrition. The lovely rice pudding always had a brown skin on top. This was my favourite part, and it tasted so rich and creamy made from the dried milk.

Sometimes, we hid meat slices in our coat pockets at school. We could ask for as much as we could eat during lunch time. The meat remained in our coats all afternoon. So it was no surprise when the whole family came down with food poisoning!

Nuns from *Little Sisters of the Poor* came around the house and took care of us. They scrubbed the place spotless and cooked up a wonderful meal each day for us hungry kids. The nuns took such good care of our family for a month until everyone felt better.

The Catholic Church provided help for poor people in need. The nuns who came to care for us were in their late 20s and 30s, very busy and efficient ladies, but so kind to us little kids.

A family moved into our neighbourhood which had no Mum. She had died and left five kids for the Dad. Within an hour, the nuns arrived to help the family. They were so wonderful.

Another time, a family was being evicted from their house for not paying the rent. Several hours later, the local priest showed up with rent money and three nuns to help take the poor family's belongings back inside the house they had been evicted from.

The sisters cooked us steak in the oven with roasties. We thought we had died and gone to heaven. Usually, we ate a lump of bread toasted by the fire with bacon grease. They cooked us a delicious tea every night they were there. The Church provided free food. So, they must have seen we had absolutely nothing in the house to eat except for bread and *Oxos*.

They also advised Lucy on how to keep food fresh. Of course, they never knew that we had been bringing our lunch meat home in our pockets. That was the end of us doing that. We were back on fried bread in bacon grease or lard.

Chapter Sixteen

The Accident
13th September 1943

A morning dove cooed happily in the sunlight, as the residents of Briarwood Road awakened. Unbeknown to her neighbors, Lucy Doyle lay on her back at the bottom of her staircase. The soft sound of the bird contrasted with the memories of that explosive night that had led her here.

On the morning they first arrived, she and Herby carried what little possessions had survived the Luftwaffe's raid, which destroyed their previous home. Lucy and Herby trekked back and forth carrying what they could salvage from the bomb site. The Jerries had taken almost everything.

"But not our lives!" Lucy said, and shook her

fist up at the sky. No longer dotted with dark, sinister warplanes and the smoke of the ack-ack guns, the daytime left them in peace to rebuild their lives. The May Blitz and the loss of her home had never really gone away. Briarwood Road was quite different from the docks where they had previously lived.

Sarah Doyle, Herbert's mother, also lived on Briarwood, unaware of the accident.

Sarah was widowed young.

Sarah, Lucy's Mother-In-Law, worked on Carnatic Drive. The house on Carnatic Drive was far different from Briarwood Road, more of a mansion with a huge piece of land. The family she worked for owned three cars and were very wealthy compared to us. Sarah came from a similar background, but my Grandad died very young.

She was a great cook, baking wonderful loaves of bread daily, steak and kidney pies, homemade soups. Sometimes we smelled the delicious food if we walked by her front door.

Sarah Doyle brought home the wealthy family's

clothes to wash, which left the scent of perfumed soap powder in the air. Silk blouses, starched white shirts, we ran our hands over the delicate fabrics and thought we could never afford to own such garments.

Heating the iron by the fire on a hot plate, my Nana pressed and smoothed the clothes for hours each day in order to put food on the table for her eight kids. Now grown up, they appreciated all she had done to keep them out of an orphanage.

Sarah was a strict Mum who stood for no nonsense. Her kids all learned good trades.

The boys were handsome with black hair, slim builds and great personalities. My Uncle Walter became an electrician. My Uncle Arthur became a carpenter. Uncle Frank emigrated to Australia at 18 and became a pilot in the war. My Dad, Herbert, became a sewing-machine mechanic and an inventor.

My Aunty Norah became a secretary. Aunty Jean was a nurse. Aunty Joan was a hairdresser. Aunty Mabel cooked at a school.

My Aunty Joan bleached her brown hair to

platinum blonde. Her sisters kept their original colours. They were pretty women. Each was tall and slender and well spoken.

Sarah was a devoted mother. The older kids would pass the younger ones over the fence so that she could nurse them and still keep working.

On that morning on Briarwood Road, Lucy Doyle had just poured warm water into a bucket, at the top of the stairs. Herby was due home on leave from the Scottish Guard in a couple of days. Taking a bar of soap to scrub down the wooden staircase, it had become much harder to clean the house, now that her belly protruded.

Herby's Mum, Sarah, had never approved of their marriage.

"She's a shop assistant," Sarah hissed at Herbert when the engagement was announced. "Your grandfather didn't work his way up to being a doctor for you to marry beneath you."

Sarah would sometimes call around to see dishes piled up in the sink, while Lucy taught her daughters the Fox Trot, tap tapping across the worn tiles of the kitchen floor. Sarah made disapproving clucking sounds with her tongue and narrowed her eyes, obsessed with speck of dust and crumb.

We were never welcome in Sarah's house as children. On some occasions, however, my Nana gave us a freshly baked biscuit or a small piece of baked bread. We were never sure if she loved us.

When Lucy crashed down the stairs that morning, tt wasn't Sarah that Lucy called for help. Slipping on the bar of soap, her pregnant body hit every wooden stair on the way down. The pain coursed through her. She bounced down to the hard bottom landing. A sticky stream of blood began to pool around Lucy, as she grasped at her belly. Her stomach pulled in tight. The contractions came in waves.

Lucy's hand grabbed at little Jean, who was two-years old. Her eyes already filled with tears at the sight of her mother.

"Go and get Mary Roberts, darlin'! Right away. Run down."

Despite her worry for her Mum, Jean was excited at being given such an important job. She skipped down to number 19 and banged at the front door with her little fists.

Jean Doyle 1943 | credit: Doreen Doyle

"Come quick. Me Mum said. She fell, and her tummy hurts."

Mary Roberts's face turned white, and she took hold of Jean's hand, calling back into her house.

"Go across the street to Mrs. Davis' phone and call the midwife," she told her daughter Maureen.

Mary knew Lucy well. As her best friend, she figured it was three months too early to give birth. She whispered a quick prayer as she raced up the street with little Jean Doyle. Mary placed clean towels under Lucy and a pillow beneath her head.

Minnie Pauls, the midwife, was dressed in a stiffly starched white skirt and blouse, carrying her bag with delivery tools inside. But by the time she joined their group at the bottom of the stairs, the baby had already been born, a skinny-malink screaming her head off.

Minnie placed the new baby onto a scale. "She's three pounds ten ounces," she said solemnly. "I wouldn't give her a name just yet, love." She embraced Lucy.

Lucy decided to just call her Baby.

Herby Doyle arrived back from London the

following morning. He had traveled all night on the train and walked the few miles from Mossley Hill station to Briarwood Road. When he entered the house and saw the new little baby girl, he was shocked how tiny she was.

After the initial shock he exclaimed, "Looks like another little blondie with pale blue eyes." Swinging Jean onto his knees, she giggled with delight. But Herby's heart dropped at Baby's tiny size. He hid his emotions behind a smile and kissed his girls.

Herby gently stroked the little face, and he wrapped his arms around Lucy.

Aunties Eileen and Gladys were there to help. The premature birth was the news of the whole street. The local MD came out the next day to check Lucy over.

Lucy tried different types of dried milk, which she received from the clinic on Lark Lane, but they were too hard for such a tiny human to tolerate. Eventually they settled on a special mixture and Baby began to thrive. The mixture had some otter's milk in it, with a nice sweet smell. Lucy mixed in sugar.

Eileen and Gladys helped her daily. Eileen immediately picked up a pile of washing and started to scrub it on the scrub board. Lucy protested, trying to sit up, but biting her lip with the pain.

"I'll be able to do it meself in no time, love." Lucy's bruises covered her backside and legs. She could barely walk.

Gladys cooked a leg of lamb for everyone, the fat sizzling as she brought it out of the oven. The smell of the succulent meat filled the tiny kitchen for several days.

Nell, arrived on Thursday. Nell was just in her early 20s, with lovely brown eyes and light brown hair. She was about five-foot seven-inches, walked with her head held high and appeared taller than she actually was. A lovely personality always ready to have a giggle and tell a joke. She pitched in right away stripping the bed and washing the sheets on the scrub-board in the back yard.

Within two weeks, Lucy was her old self again,

coping wonderfully with her two little daughters. It turned out that the scrawny premature baby was tougher than anyone had expected. As Baby gained weight and kicked her chubby legs at the house guests, she was eventually given a name: Doreen. It was me.

As I grew larger my nickname became "Our Do."

Aigburth Vale was a lovely section of Liverpool, with its hedge-lined houses. Some people had little rows of flowers in front of their house, adding a colourful touch. A classic middle-class area, all the houses were very neat and clean, built from different shades of bricks, with coping stones around the front windows.

Briarwood Road ended quietly with only two cars on the entire street. Hedges were so tall around front windows that they provided privacy.

Children played on the street all day when there was no School. So the neighbourhood was filled with happy little kids despite the war.

Most Briarwood homes were two-up/two-down tiny places. None featured a bathroom inside or running hot water. The upper middle class areas had three bedrooms / one bathroom. After World War Two the houses were all updated. Eventually everyone had an inside bathroom and toilet.

Gladys came round to visit the new baby, and she usually brought pictures and letters that Tom Whitney had sent her from the war.

The family was overjoyed to see photos of him with his little brother Jack. They were both very much in peril fighting at sea. Stationed on ships in the Atlantic, the Mediterranean, and eventually the Pacific, the Whitney men had gone on leave together in Singapore. In photos they were dressed in khaki shorts, and my Uncle Tom was holding his little dog. They were still doing smashing after four years of combat on the high seas, first against the Germans and now the Japanese.

Tom Whitney wrote that he found a little stray dog and adopted it, sneaking it onto various ships inside his kit bag. His shipmates were made up and held a raffle to choose a name for it. Finally, they settled on Lassie.

These letters kept everyone from focusing on the horrors of the war in the Pacific and at home. The nightly bombings might have stopped, but the city was splintered. Piles of rubble lined the roads. Houses that had been cut in half still displayed remnants of the lives once lived there. The smell of smoke and burning lingered in the air.

As the days moved on, more of Gladys' letters were read, photos pored over and meals cooked.

After Herby left to return to his unit, my Aunties took turns coming over to care for my Mum, along with her wonderful neighbours, who cooked meals for her and Jean.

Briarwood Road was never bombed. Thank God. The city's center received the majority of the bombing raids.

Sarah Doyle, my Nana apparently did come to visit me when I was a newborn. She did not help my Mum in her recovery. Only my Mum's sisters and my

Aunty Gladys helped her, as well as Mary Roberts from down the street, and also Mrs. Sargent from three houses away. Ny Nana only lived down the street, and so I found that very unsettling as I grew older.

One time, when I was a teenager, I rode my bike nine miles from our new house in Speke to visit my Nana. She was quite old, and I hadn't seen her prior for five years. I rode with my friend Yvonne.

For the very first time, Sarah was glad to see me. She was by now quite old and sick. She made us both cups of tea, and she gave us some of her lovely homemade shortbread biscuits. Those melted in your mouth, all buttery. We talked for over an hour

Sarah Doyle died not long afterwards. So I was glad I'd taken time out to go and see her that day.

The Luftwaffe bombing of Liverpool had stopped, and so the Mums on the street enjoyed long walks in magnificent Sefton Park, several blocks away. Endless scenic paths led to the Fairy Glen and the Palm House.

Sefton Park was a heavenly retreat. The Mums

gathered and walked around the beautiful lake, watching swans glide effortlessly through the water. They often took a picnic with them, and sat on the grass slopes by the lake enjoying the lovely views.

The Palm House was so beautiful early on in the war, until it was bombed by the Germans and almost totally destroyed. Most people were completely devastated when they saw all the pointless damage. Years later, the Palm House was restored, and today beautiful wedding receptions are held there.

Younger kids loved the Fairy Glen. We would bring empty jam jars and scoop up tadpoles, often taking care of them until they became frogs. Then we took them back and released them. It was pretty in the Autumn when we gathered conkers and acorns, climbing up the rocks, just sheer joy for little children.

Chapter Seventeen

A Wartime Christmas

W ith all the devastation and uncertainty that the war brought, Christmas was difficult. The Mums of the family always did their best to make sure their kids felt the season was special.

Aunty Eileen announced, "Let's take them all down to the Grotto and let them see Father Christmas."

"Mine talk about it every day," said Gladys.

"When do yer want to go?" asked Nell.

They decided on a day they hoped wouldn't be too crowded. Everyone brought butties and water. The kids' faces lit up at the magical trees, sparkly lights, and the main attraction Father Christmas. The Grotto was decorated with fluffy artificial snow and lots of twinkling lights in all different colours that kept them wide-eyed. The little ones were speechless. Happy Christmas music played. The family was so thrilled, it was like landing in a new world, compared to the rest of the city.

The children knew well not to ask for too much. Rationing was so strict and money scarce. A coloring book and some colored pencils were popular choices. Gladys let on to Father Christmas that was what she would be getting them.

Afterwards, they sat on a wall by the *Adelphi Hotel* and ate their spam, egg, and jam butties. Lots of *Rolls-Royces* parked in front of the hotel. Ladies in full-length fur coats and gentlemen in tuxedos strolled inside.

Our group had never seen anything like it before. The hotel's staff came over to the cars and carried in the huge suitcases, as the guests strutted past and up to the cavernous front entrance. The *Adelphi* lobby was decorated in Christmas garland.

The kids had finally seen Father Christmas and

now they were witnessing all these rich and famous people. As they watched from the wall enjoying their butties, it was like going to the pictures. They talked about it for weeks.

The kids were excited to put their order in for Christmas presents. Shivering a bit in the breeze from the River Mersey, they linked arms to stay warm as they strolled back to Gladys's house.

Gladys heated them a pot of tea and offered *Marie Biscuits*. They were little biscuits, which most people dipped into their cups of tea. These were so tasty because of the sweet vanilla flavouring.

Herby Doyle was a skilled guitar teacher, and he taught for many years. Sid, his band member, often came over when Herby was back on leave, and their little band played out at the local pubs.

During his Christmas leave, they managed to get together for a couple of good parties and sing-alongs with Herby playing. The ladies of the family were so happy he was back at the same time as Tom Whitney.

Sometimes when Herby practiced in the house with Sid, several neighbors would gather outside 53 Briarwood and dance the quick step or jitterbug or one of the latest dance styles. They were mostly local Mums happy to have a bit of fun in spite of the endless war. Herby was great at playing popular big band songs.

Chapter Eighteen

The Bomb

The bloody war dragged on. Tom hadn't been able to return home and see his family for two years. He arrived back in Liverpool in 1944 with one of his shipmates, Billy Riley, who happened to be a bomb expert. The two sailors had been serving with Captain Johnny Walker in the Battle of the Atlantic.

When they walked into Tom and Gladys' parlor, Billy Riley spotted little Peter's bomb trophy sitting on display on the mantle.

"What the hell is that?" he shouted. "Get out! All of yis. Fast hurry. Bang on the neighbors as well and run across the street!"

Everyone was taken by surprise.

"What's going on?" shouted little Peter.

"Yer Dad's mate said we 'ave to get out," said Gladys.

The seven-year-old Peter said, "I hope they aren't messing with me bomb."

Police arrived within five minutes and blocked off the entire street.

Billy McGuire, from the house opposite, asked, "What's 'appening, lad?" Billy was also home on leave after serving with Tom and Billy in the Atlantic campaign. His wife Jean held their new baby.

"Dunno. Me Dad's mate has gone daft."

After 45 minutes the bomb squad arrived.

People from all over the neighborhood formed a crowd causing a sensation on Woodruff Street. The bomb squad worked in the house for almost an hour. When they emerged, carrying a big metal box, Peter shouted at them, "Where's me bomb?"

The man in charge said, "It's in here, lad. Yis are all lucky it never went off."

"I thought it was a dud," replied Peter.

So did everyone else in the family. They all believed the bomb was a dud.

"Naaah. How long did you have it, lad?"

"Mmm, since 1941. May I think."

"Well, all I can say is yer all very lucky." The man drove off with Peter's prized possession. He watched them leave, knowing he would miss all the attention.

Billy Riley strolled over. "Don't feel bad. Aren't yer glad no one got hurt, lad?"

"I suppose. I'll 'ave to start all over again now looking fer treasure." Only small fragments of shrapnel remained. The big bomb had been found right after the Blitz.

Peter decided he would try going over to Denton Street. Lads spent endless hours searching for pieces of bombs and other war treasures to show each other and compete over who had the best find.

Tom Whitney felt bad that his boy had lost his treasured bomb. To cheer him up he came up with an idea.

"I tell yer what, lad. Come Sundee I'll take yer up to Aunty Eils and we will take yis all on the lake at Sefton Park. I'll get us a rowboat, fer you and the other kids."

Peter was overjoyed. Trips were rare. He couldn't wait, and he told all his mates as they searched for more shrapnel they might have missed.

Sunday morning, the kids were up at the crack of dawn, happy to have their Dad back on leave. Lucy came over with Herbert, who also had a few days leave, and us kids.

The Dads rowed the boats around the lake. Peter had a chance to row as well as Fred. Up the lake they went to the little Island in the middle, then back down the other side. The kids felt so happy splashing their hands in the water and escaping from the war. The row boats were about 12-foot long, wooden vessels, with one set of oars. About six people fit into each one, and you rented it by the hour, enough time to row up the lake and return down to the dock.

All around the lake kids and dads fished. Some

kids had fashioned rods from branches with strings attached. Mums walked their babies in high prams all around the lake.

Tom Whitney and a shipmate | credit: Peter Whitney

When the rowboats returned to shore, the families moved up to a grassy slope by the boat house and had their picnic. An ice-cream truck had parked at the park's entrance. The Dads decided that the kids could all have a lolly ice.

"Wow!" they screamed. They couldn't believe

their luck, a boat ride and a lolly ice. This was the best day out ever.

Tom remained home with Gladys for just another two days. Then it was time for him to ship out again. The kids, Peter and Jeanie, were especially upset to lose their father again.

Tom instructed them, "Be brave. Take care of yer Mam."

Tom Whitney's battle photos | credit: Peter Whitney

He shipped out on the HMS *Starling*. This was a

sloop of the modified *Black Swan* class. It specialized in hunting submarines. The aircraft carrier HMS *Illustrious* was being repaired. So, Tom was deployed to HMS *Formidable*. This was an aircraft carrier of the *Illustrious* class, launched in August 1939.

Tom Whitney's battle photos | credit: Peter Whitney

She was to accompany a convoy to Capetown, S. Africa, but was called to the Mediterranean to replace Tom's previous ship HMS *Illustrious*, which had been severely damaged. Tom Whitney served on her for about six months.

The *Formidable* supported Crete operations in May, 1941, where she suffered serious damage from air attacks with 1000kg bombs. *Formidable* was out of action for six months, when she underwent repairs in America and then joined the Eastern Fleet in the Indian ocean in 1942.

Tom's Pacific battle photos | credit: Peter Whitney

The HMAS *Arunta* and HMAS *Warramunga*

were part of the covering force. They shelled Japanese military positions on the shores and protected landing craft, as those carried infantry soldiers to their designated landing beaches at Leyte Gulf in the Philippines.

The massive Battle of Leyte Gulf finished off the Japanese Navy as a capable fighting force. Tom was one of the brave gunners who fought in this battle.

Chapter Nineteen

Peter in Hospital

Peter Whitney fell sick and barely able to move. Three other kids in Peter's class had recently died of diphtheria.

Gladys called for an ambulance, and they carried Peter out of the house on a stretcher. The ambulance cost was relatively low at that time, and the hospital costs were paid on a weekly payment plan. Often people paid over years to cover the costs of treatment.

Peter then spent the next sixteen weeks in the hospital. He contracted meningitis as well as diphtheria, and he had to have spinal taps. Through his many injections and blood tests he remained a little trooper.

His Dad was away at sea on HMS *Illustrious*.

Gladys, Eileen, Nellie, and Lucy visited him on a regular basis. Gladys' Mam and her Sisters would sit with the kids when they were needed.

By his second week in hospital, Peter hated everything about being sick.

The nurse took Gladys aside. "He won't eat," she said. "He keeps refusing."

Gladys sat to have a talk with him. "How are yer, lad?"

"I hate it 'ere."

"Never mind. What yer want for tea?"

"Ice cream!" said Peter.

"Okay then," said his Mam. "Ice cream it is. I'll be right back."

Peter couldn't believe his luck, getting what he had demanded.

Gladys shot down to the first floor and asked the receptionist, "Do yer know where I can get a *Walls Bar?*"

"Down Smithdown Road, love," the receptionist said. "Three blocks on the corner is a tobacconist."

Gladys ran down to the shop as fast as she could.

"I'll 'ave a *Walls Bar* please," she said to the owner.

The man smiled.

Back in hospital, Peter gloated. "Me Mam's bringing me an ice cream."

The stern-looking Matron wasn't impressed. "An ice cream is it? And that will be yer tea?"

"Aye," said Peter.

Gladys came rushing in.

"There yer go, lad."

The Matron's face was horrified.

Gladys didn't care. He could have whatever he wanted, as long as he ate something. This went on for the duration of his hospitalization. Sometimes Peter wanted a chip butty. Sometimes beans on toast. Whatever he wanted to eat, Gladys tried her best to acquire.

Peter's condition slowly improved. Because Gladys knew best for her little seven-year-old lad, he survived the diphtheria. His hair grew very long being in hospital for all those weeks.

"Yer look like a little girl," said his Mum.

He got mad, shouting at her, "I'm not a girl!"

Finally, after four months, Peter grew well enough to leave Smithdown hospital and head home. Gladys picked him up, and they rode the tram back to Park Road. He looked fit and handsome, far different from the sick little boy she had sent to the hospital all those weeks ago. Gladys was so happy to have her little lad home again. First thing she did was take him to the barber shop to get his curly locks cut.

Chapter Twenty

HMS Illustrious

The *Liverpool Echo* posted war news every day. A headline from the paper read:

HMS Illustrious bombed by the Luftwaffe

HMS Illustrious under attack on 10th January 1941

Tom was in this battle. After his time with Captain Johnny Walker in the Atlantic campaign, Tom developed far greater skills as a gun-layer. His superiors assigned him to the HMS *Illustrious*, the massive aircraft carrier. There he skillfully manned the guns during many battles. Tom was involved with action in the Mediterranean Sea.

Tom also found time to take pictures with his new brownie camera. He brought them home to show Gladys on his next leave. His family treasured them all for the next seventy plus years. They meant so much to the family, Tom taking all these photos as the battles raged on in front of him.

Tom Whitney's battle photos from HMS Illustrious | credit: Peter Whitney

On the picture below he wrote, "This one was bit closer than I liked, but a good picture though."

Tom wrote comments on most of the photos, some quite comical. He would say, "This guy has along swim home," as a pilot was drifting down with his parachute.

Tom Whitney's battle photos from Illustrious | credit: Peter Whitney

In this battle, German dive-bombers severely damaged the *Illustrious*. It took six direct bomb hits and several near misses, which caused fires and disabled the steering.

The casualties were 83 killed, 80 seriously wounded, and 40 slightly wounded. HMS *Warspite* also sustained damage from a near miss. During this attack one Fulmar fighter and one Swordfish torpedo planes were shot down, with their crews being saved. Two enemy aircraft were also shot down by gunfire.

Tom Whitney's battle photos from Illustrious | credit: Peter Whitney

Also, the HMS *Valiant* suffered one killed and three wounded from the near misses.

Tom Whitney's battle photos from Illustrious | credit: Peter Whitney

At 13:30, an unsuccessful attack was made on *Illustrious* by high altitude bombers. A second attack with 30 Luftwaffe dive bombers targeted the surrounding fleet. A bomb struck the *Illustrious*.

Fulmar fighters from the *Illustrious*, which had refueled in Malta, shot down six or seven German planes and damaged several others.

Tom (top left) with shipmates | credit: Peter Whitney

Sadly, Tom's little dog Lassie, which he had kept for the past few years, was hit by a piece of shrapnel and died instantly. She apparently had escaped the latrine where she was kept during raids. It was a huge loss to the crew.

Two of Tom's good friends were also killed in this battle.

The *Illustrious*, covered by the fleet, escaped to the port at Malta. Just outside the entrance to the Grand Harbour, another attack by torpedo bombers was fought off and the Luftwaffe failed to sink her. Eleven Swordfish torpedo planes and five more Fulmar fighters were lost in the fires.

Repairs of the ship were carried out In Malta. HMS *Illustrious* then returned to Alexandria, Egypt despite further Luftwaffe attacks. In Egypt, the *Illustrious* was fixed sufficiently to take the Suez Canal and head south around Africa and back to the U.S. shipyards of Norfolk Virginia. She sat in dock for the remainder of that year.

Tom was redeployed to the HMS *Cleopatra*, a

Dido class cruiser launched in March of 1940. This ship was attacked from the air during entry into the Maltese Grand Harbour in February 1942. Hit by a 500kg bomb, which exploded and caused sustained flooding, she was taken in for repairs at the Malta shipyards.

Tom went over to the HMS *Formidable*, and he was involved in operations off Madagascar in April 1942.

Tom Whitney would go on to eventually be so good as a gun-layer that he was transferred to the HMAS *Warramunga*, an Australian battleship, and shipped to the coast of Japan to shoot down Kamikazes. The Kamikaze fighters were devastating, as they piloted their planes straight down into the ships, killing themselves in the attack. These were both guided missiles and suicide bombers. Tom was very lucky for a while.

It appears from the letters we have, that his final battle was on the HMS *Penn*, where he was severely injured and nearly died. Tom was serving in the British Pacific Fleet operations off the coast of Japan, and there is a mention of Kure.

Tom Whitney's naval career spanned six years of non-stop war and numerous, major sea battles.

His brother, Jack Whitney, was also involved in many of the large battles as a gunner, and he luckily escaped physical injury through the remainder of the war. Jack's injuries were psychological.

When Jack was younger, he would often break down and cry, remembering his best friend who had pulled the plug on his life vest. He felt so terrible that he had been unable to convince his mate to stick it out. As life passed by, Jack became an alcoholic.

The two Whitney brothers were truly courageous, ordinary men. I'm so proud that they were my uncles.

Chapter Twenty One

Victory

On V-E Day, May 8th, 1945, U.K. Prime Minister Winston Churchill broadcast the news that the war with Germany was over. He waved at the celebrating crowds in Whitehall, London. Piccadilly Circus was overrun with thousands and thousands of frenzied celebrators. People ran up to total strangers and hugged and kissed them. They literally danced in the streets, so relieved and happy it was all over.

On April 30th Adolf Hitler committed suicide in his bunker in Berlin. Germany surrendered, authorized by his successor, Reichspräsident Karl Dönitz. This administration was known as the Flensburg Government. The military surrender was

signed on May 7th in Reims, France and on May 8th in
Berlin.

The people of Liverpool held street parties to
celebrate the end of the war. With donated food from
neighbors and lots of jelly and custard, what joy to us
little kids who prior had nothing much to eat for
years.

Festivals were organized with sack races and
fun and games. It was a truly unforgettable day.
Starving kids now had food galore, jelly and custard
with lovely raspberry flavour, sausage rolls with
heavenly flaky crust, and sandwiches, as many as you
could eat. From lumps of white bread toasted by the
fire to all this delicious feast, it was just overwhelming
for us kids.

My Mum, Lucy, saw a sign in Sefton Park that
they were going to hold concerts each Sunday, and
there would be talent competitions for the children.
Each age group could participate. We were over the
moon with excitement. It was like nothing we'd ever
experienced in our lives. There was a stage with

dressing rooms, and it was all fenced around in a circle. You had to pay if you wern't a performer, usually six-pence. It drew a variety of acts, tap dancers, gymnasts, singers, and kids like us playing musical instruments and dancing.

Lucy was friends with Sid's fiancé, Mary, who was from the Philippines. She offered to loan Lucy two lovely grass skirts for myself and my sister Jean to wear in the talent competition.

Herby bought us girls a ukulele each and taught us three notes. We learned to do a hula dance with Mum's help.

On the day of the big competition, we were up at six am. Lucy dabbed liquid coffee all over us to add tan. She made us both flowered garlands. These had the most wonderful smell of spring flowers. She also clipped huge artificial flowers to our heads.

As we trekked through Sefton Park, with baby Frank in his pram, everyone complimented us on how great we looked. Inside the concert, we sat in the front row waiting for the other acts to finish. Then we went up on stage and did our little hula dance, as Mum coached us from the side, swinging her hips.

The Doyle sisters played our three notes on the ukuleles.

"Aloha Hawaii..." and the crowd went wild.

We received second place that day and I'm sure the competition was rigged. The organizers' kids happened to win. We did win a nice coloring book each, though, but not the gigantic jigsaw puzzle.

Chapter Twenty Two

Fourth Birthday Party

On my fourth birthday, in 1947, my mum went all out to throw me a wonderful party. She cooked jelly and custard. Mary Roberts came by to help her ice the Queen Cakes. They spread margarine and ham paste on the butties. What a treat for us. Our mouths watered at the thought of that lovely feast.

Mum even bought us a bottle of lemonade for everyone to have a sweet drink. It was a gorgeous sunny day.

I saw our neighbor Phyllis across the street. She lived with her sister Flo, two nice older ladies. I used to talk to them all the time. They took turns scrubbing the front doorstep each day.

"Can I go see Phyllis, Mum?" I asked.

"Okay darlin'. Don't stay too long." My Mum
replied.

All my best mates were coming over shortly.
Maureen and Lynne Roberts, Mary's two girls, and
Joan Sargent who lived at number 61, along with Janet
Ferguson who lived opposite. Such excitement!

I ran over to tell Phyllis that it was my
birthday. She was such a warm person, and she gave
me a big hug. A sweet lady with silver hair pulled back
in a bun, she stood tall and thin with deep blue eyes.

"Wait a minute, Do. I have something for you."

I stood in shock. We never received presents
from anyone. Phyllis returned with a little ballerina
statue in blue-colored glass. I was so thrilled, I hugged
her again and ran back across to show Mum.

As I crossed the street, I fell down and the little
statue broke. A piece of the glass embedded in my
knee. The pain was unbearable,and my knee was
throbbing so badly and I could barely walk.

When my Mum saw me injured she began to

cry . My friends were arriving. Mum tried her best to make light of it.

"Be brave, love. I'll dig it out," she said. Then she whispered in my ear, "You can say any swear word you like while I dig out this glass."

What a surprise!

As my Mum poked a big needle into my knee to remove the glass shard, I shouted, "Bugger off! Swines! Sod off!" And finally, "Shit shit shit!"

My friends' eyes went big as saucers.

"Go on, love," Mum encouraged me.

She dug deeply into my knee and worked out the embedded piece of glass. It was soon bandaged up, and the party continued.

We ate our goodies and played lots of games. Whenever I see that scar on my knee, I remember that day so vividly, exactly how my Mum was. She was able to take any situation from awful to easily coped with. Lucy had so many funny expressions she would often make a joke at otherwise serious situations.

If the food looked off, Lucy said, "Shite of the

highest order." She said, "Ladies and gentlemen take my advice, pull down your knickers and slide on the ice."

We screeched with laughter.

If Mum didn't believe a story someone was telling she would speak up immediately and say, "It sounds like a bucket of shit from China to me, a bit far fetched." We would all crack up laughing.

One day, we all walked home from school through Sefton Park. I was five. My sister was seven, and Frank was a baby in his pram. As we approached the Palm House, suddenly a strange man jumped out from behind a tree with his willy out.

Us girls were stunned and petrified, but not my Mum.

Lucy wasn't a bit concerned as we clung onto her. She told him, "You soft swine."

The flasher wound up totally deflated and scurried off.

As innocent small children, we had no idea what the "bad man" was doing, so we interpreted it as him trying to scare us with a big stick. Mum made us feel like he was just a silly man, and perhaps he was. We told all our friends how he had tried to scare us but our Mum wasn't scared.

Lucy told everyone, "Apparently his stick wasn't as big as he thought."

It became a family joke, and we didn't know why until we grew up and realized the implications of the event. Mum had protected us.

Chapter Twenty Three

Tom's Long Journey Home

I t appears that Tom Whitney was involved in a battle that raged for over seven hours, where Kamikazes attempted to crash into the ship. They flew to a high altitude and dove straight down at the deck. These were incredibly difficult for the gunners to stop.

One of the Japanese planes made it through the anti-aircraft fire. In the explosion, flying metal shrapnel hit the left side of Tom's skull and sliced off a section. This could have been instantly fatal.

A lot of his mates were killed that day, but Tom was lucky. He lay in sick bay as they sailed back to Egypt. The HMS *Penn* was now assisting with salvage operations. So many ships were crippled and falling apart.

Amid this mess, Tom Whitney was transferred to a hospital ship, the *Nieuw Amsterdam*. This luxury cruise liner had been seized by the allies from Holland when the Germans invaded and took over that country.

Tom's battle photographs | credit: Peter Whitney

Once a luxurious ocean liner with huge crystal chandeliers and plush carpeting throughout, the *Nieuw Amsterdam* had been stripped down to the bare necessities in order to fit as many injured men as possible. They were crammed in like sardines.

Some, like Tom, were severely hurt. Others less critical. Those not too badly injured would pass the time reading paperbacks and playing cards. With barely enough room to squeeze into the bunks, and the floors were coated with vomit and diarrhea. The stench throughout the ship was unbearable. The lucky ones slept.

Tom Whitney was placed into a medically induced coma for the first five days after his surgery. On day six he was able to talk to some of his shipmates and play a few hands of cards.

Storms assaulted the *Nieuw Amsterdam* for nine days as it cruised on its long journey. The ship rocked from side to side continually. Men hung over the rails vomiting. Sailors who were not too severely injured had the job of burying the dead overboard. They also mopped the vomit-covered floors.

Eventually, the *Nieuw Amsterdam* arrived in Egypt. The temperature was over 90 degrees.

Tom was possibly transferred over to the HMS

George V to head back to England, but the records are sketchy. What's clear is that after six years and numerous battles, it seemed incredible to suffer this terrible injury in just the last few days of the war.

Gladys received a letter that told how he had been injured. She was frantic with worry.

Tom's head was patched up with a piece of steel implanted in his skull. This closed up the hole left by the flying shrapnel. He suffered pain from this head trauma for the remainder of his life.

Tom finally arrived back in England. He was kept heavily sedated so that he could heal. Once the ship docked, Tom asked one of his shipmates to allow him to borrow his ID papers. Thus, he was able to travel back home and reunite with Gladys and the kids.

She prepared a lovely dinner, his favorite, Scouse. After a quiet meal, she and Tom walked up to the corner pub to catch up on all they had missed.

Tom needed to return to the ship by seven am the following day. But he was overjoyed to finally make it back to Liverpool with his family after everything he had endured.

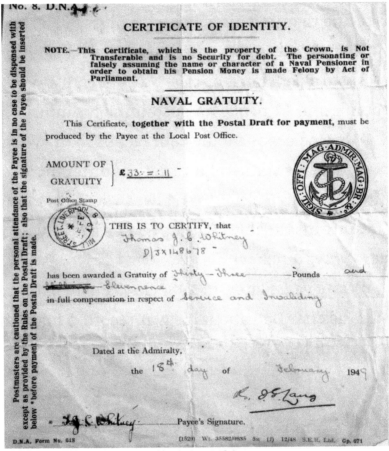

Credit: Peter Whitney

Despite his head injury, Tom Whitney

remained proud of his exemplary war record. His wound caused him chronic pain. He spent the rest of his life, after working all day, hanging out in the local pubs trying to numb his aches with pints of ale.

Tom Whitney was discharged on a disability. He received a pension from the Navy and an award of 33 pounds and 11 pence for sustaining his injuries.

My Uncle was a truly courageous man, who worked until his sixties at a variety of different jobs, despite his severed skull. Tom always kept his family fed. Despite his terrible trauma, he was a lovely happy Uncle, always quick with a joke.

Many years later, in 1980, my cousin Barbara wrote to ask her Dad about his war record. This is the letter he sent her:

I'VE INCLUDED THIS TO
SHOW YOU MY IN-
DEPTH KNOWLEDGE OF
HIS SHIPS.

290 QUEENS DRIVE
WALTON
LIVERPOOL 4
8SL
26/10/80

My dear Barbara we got your letter
and your Mam asked me to write
to you. I hope you and the kids
are well, also Joop, when you write
to him tell him I wish him well.
You asked me to give you the
names of the ships I served in
while in the Navy, well Tommy has
a big job because I served and
fought on a lot. I'll try my best
to remember them or most of them
so here goes. HMS EAGLE TRAINING SHIP.
HMS DRAKE ROYAL NAVAL BARRACKS DEVONPORT
PLYMOUTH. HMS BRITTOMART FLEET MINE SWEEPER
HMS VINTY DESTROYER 4 4.5" GUNS 4
TWIN MACHINE GUNS 8 TORPEDO TUBES.
HMS WESSEX DESTROYER 4 4-5" GUNS
4 TWIN MACHINE GUNS 8 TORPEDO TUBES
HMS BEAUFORT FLEET SURVEY SHIP.
HMS MISTRAL DESTROYER 4 4-5" GUNS
8 TORPEDO TUBES. 4 TWIN MACHINE GUNS.
HMS ILLUSTRIOUS FLEET AIRCRAFT CARRIER
CARRIED 20 FIGHTERS 18 TORPEDO BOMBERS
CARRIED 2000 OFFICERS AND MEN
WAR COMPLIMENT ARMAMENT WAS 16 4-45
ACK ACK GUNS ANTI AIR CRAFT IN 8 TURRETS
AND 4 CHICAGO PIANOS 8 BARRELS POM POMS
HEAVY MACHINE GUNS

(2)

HMS CARLISLE ANTI AIRCRAFT CRUISER
GRANDAD WAS GUNLAYER ON THE MISHIP
TWIN 4.5 INCH GUNS WE GOT SEVEN GERMAN
DIVE BOMBERS STUKA 87s AND 88s
THE SHIPS GUNS HELPED THEM TO KEEP DIVING
GOOD.
HMS CLEOPATRA FLEET CRUISER ANTI AIRCRAFT
10 5.25ins GUNS 3 TURRETS FORWARD AND
2 TURRETS AFT 10 TWIN ORLICKANS
HEAVY MACHINE GUNS 8 TORPEDO TUBES
100 DEPTH CHARGES SAME AS HMS CARLISLE
HMS MEDWAY SUBMARINE DEPOT SHIP
12 TWIN 4.5ins GUNS 12 ORLICKANS
200 TORPEDO'S FOR THE SUBS AND ALL
SPARE PARTS.
HMS FORMIDABLE FLEET AIRCRAFT CARRIER
SAME GUNS AS ILLUSTRIOUS
LANDED ME AT SINGAPORE
HMS WARRAMUNGA AUSTRALIAN DESTROYER
TOOK ME TO KURE JAPAN
HMS PENN DESTROYER 4.4.5in GUNS
8 TORPEDO TUBES 8 ORLICKANS
180 SHIPS CREWE
CAME HOME FROM JAPAN INVALIDED HOME
ON THE NEW AMSTERDAM TO PORT TEWFICK
IN ESYPT. WHERE I HAD TO COME HOME
ON THE GEORGE. WE TIED UP AT
LANDING STAGE AND ONE OF THE CREW
LENT ME HIS SUIT AND PASS TO GET
HOME FOR THE NIGHT. I CHANGED INTO
OTHER CLOTHES AND TOOK THE OTHER
CREW MANS CLOTHES AND PASS BACK
AT SEVEN IN THE MORNING. HE WAS WHAT

Chapter Twenty four

Jean's Gang

One pleasant sunny morning in 1946, Mum braided Jean's hair for her first day at school. She was to attend *St. Anne's* across from the *People's Hall*, which was a lovely little school, protestant denomination, but they accepted Jean despite us being Catholic.

As we walked down Briarwood, I cried. I was only three and my big sister was heading off to school without me. We pushed our Frank in his pram.

Jean was the leader of our street. In order to have any fun you had to join her "gang." My Mum forced her to take me along, so that I had a playmate. Once out of her sight, Jean would concoct tests and trials in order for other kids to join her gang. These were too hard for me. I was disqualified and sent back home. Or else she would punch me in the stomach for failing. I tried so hard to do the increasingly dangerous initiation tests and be part of her gang.

At the top of our street was a factory. This building was once a mansion, a huge place with acres of land that stored war materials. The inside of the mansion had been converted with conveyor belts to move merchandise along. A war-surplus dump had been abandoned.

Sometimes Jean's tests would include jumping from the top of a pallet of goods over to a second. Since I was younger, my legs were too short. All of Jean's followers had no trouble making it across the pallets.

I ran across the stack and tried to reach the second one, but I only made it across to the edge, grabbing on for dear life.

"Too bad. You didn't make my gang today. Tara!" Jean shouted and off they all went laughing.

As I hung there, a factory worker came over and lifted me down.

"That's a very dangerous game you're playing,"

he said.

I knew that the tests to join her gang were too difficult for me, but I was determined to join in and have fun rather than be left sitting on the doorstep listening to the neighbors' gossip.

One day, Jean got a fresh idea.

The gang shimmied up on top of the wall at the back of the factory. It was cement-covered with sharp jagged glass embedded, exactly to keep us kids out. I managed to climb it too, hoping I'd passed the test. My knees were scraped and one was bleeding, but I knew if I complained I would be sent home as a wimp, too weak to join in the gang.

"Now hop along the wall on one leg!" Jean demanded.

I did try. It was impossible, and I fell off the wall into a huge covered roof.

I could hear a gigantic saw underneath me. The roaring sound from the cutting was deafening. It may have been ripping long wooden boards.

I was so lucky that I didn't go through the tent

canvas. By the time I pulled myself up, my sister's "gang" had left without me again.

It seemed like Jean seldom did the tests herself but made everyone else do them. This went on throughout our childhood, but I always loved my sister, so I desperately wanted to make it into her gang.

That huge mansion turned factory was called the *Old Brew*. We all went up the *Old Brew* on a Saturday afternoon. There was a massive, deep quarry filled with soot. All the way down the sides thick ivy grew. Jean's test this day was that you had to climb down it from 30-feet up, then swing yourself into her secret cave carved into the side of the quarry wall.

After several attempts, I was finally able to do it. So, she allowed me to spend several hours with her in the cave. I was sworn to secrecy to never tell anyone where it was. This secret place was located halfway down the quarry wall, covered in very thick foliage, so it was hard to find.

Mum and Dad would have had a fit if they had

seen us playing like that in the dangerous quarry.

Sometimes other friends visited, and they might end up victims of Jean's challenges. Mary Foo, Sid's fiance, came by with her two gorgeous nieces dressed to kill in genuine Scottish kilts. We had never seen such lovely clothes.

Mum said, "Take the girls with you two and show them your play sites." One of the girls had a red tartan kilt and sash over her shoulder. Her sister wore a yellow tartan kilt, also with sash. These were new, stunning outfits.

Jean led us up Briarwood Road, and then she announced, "You'll have to pass the test to see me best hiding cave."

The two girls were about seven. They agreed. "Okay. What do we have to do?"

"First of all," said Jean, "you have to climb over this wall covered in broken glass.

They both climbed up, and we helped them shimmy over. It was very obvious that they had never climbed anything before. We struggled to lift them both over the wall. Both of us had to push.

We Doyle girls were tomboys, but the new girls were not. Their lovely black patent leather shoes were scraped up from climbing.

Next, we arrived at the quarry site.

"To see me best cave, you have to climb down this vine. I'll bet neither of you can do it," Jean said, with her arms crossed.

"Oh we can," they said.

So, the two struggled down the hanging ivy. As they tried to swing into the secret cave, they slipped one by one completely down the side of the quarry wall, and landed in a jutting pile of soot.

We froze in terror.

"Hold on!" Jean yelled. "I'll save you."

She knew that we were in deep trouble getting those two girls completely messed up, with black marks all over their fancy new outfits.

Jean and I dusted the soot off of them as best we could, which wasn't very well. Jean then decided to tell a good story when we arrived home, or we would be getting the belt tonight. We decided to say how it was their idea to climb down the quarry, not ours.

Lucy's and Mary's faces were priceless when they got a look at us trudging down Briarwood Road. Those two lovely little girls were caked in black soot all over their expensive clothes.

"How did this happen?" asked Mary.

Jean took charge. "We tried to tell them it was dangerous. Didn't we, Do?"

I just nodded my head, not wanting to end up on Jean's bad side.

My Dad was furious with us. Sid was his favorite band member and these were his girls with scuffed shoes and ruined clothes, an expensive mistake.

Mum grabbed two of our outfits, which were homemade, and she helped wash the grimy kids. They changed into our clothes.

We kids all played up at the *Old Brew*, which was massive, opening boxes of treasures from parachutes to hand grenades. The parachutes were made of silky material, maybe silk, and perfect for twirly skirts. They felt so smooth as we ran our fingers down them.

The hand grenades were of dark green plastic. We sniffed them at first, and they all seemed fine. We took the grenades home and showed Dad. He was happy we'd found something to burn on the fire to keep us warm.

"Suffering Jesus," said Herby. "Is there a lot of them love?"

"Yeah, Dad," said Jean. "Tons stacked high."

"Well we'll be having a bloody good fire tonight," he said excitedly. "'Ere take me hammer with the claw end. You and our Do take yer Mum's shopping bags and fill em up. Use the claw end to break the locks open. Then get as many as you can carry."

He tossed the first grenade onto the fire. It gave a whoosh.

"Oh, Jesus, Herby. What is that?" Lucy came rushing in.

"It's a bleeding hand grenade," Herby said.

"Perfectly safe. They've been sitting there for years."

The house was freezing each night when the fire ran down, so it may have clouded his judgment on the matter just a little.

We were ready to head out again in the cold.

"Go on then you two. Yer can 'ave some cocoa when yer get back."

Jean and I marched straight up the *Old Brew* and climbed through the fence. We located the surplus boxes. It had snowed overnight, so a lot of them were covered with ice. Neither of us had gloves. Very soon our hands froze, trying to break open the hand grenade boxes with Dad's hammer.

I wanted to just go home, but Jean insisted we dig one more box full.

"If we get enough," she said, "me dad might give us a fire upstairs in the bedroom."

"OK." I agreed reluctantly. My finger was bleeding from digging them out with my bare hands. The pain got so severe I started to cry.

"Shurrup," Jean said. "The watchman will hear

you."

"Me hand's bleeding."

Jean grabbed her hanky. "Wrap this on it and shut yer gob," she said. "We're almost done. me Dad will be made up!"

When we arrived back at the hole in the fence we shoved the shopping bags full of hand grenades through. Then we wriggled through and headed down the road.

Young Janet Ferguson, who lived opposite us, said "What you got there?"

"Hand grenades," we said. "our Dad's burning them."

Janet was taken aback. "Me Mum said they're dangerous."

Janet was a very pretty girl, the same age as me. She had flaxen hair all curly and shoulder length, with pale blue eyes. She had a hard time keeping up with some of Jean's games. Sometimes she had difficulty catching her breath as she suffered from a heart problem. We played less strenuous games with her.

She said, "We're going to Sefton Park once it gets a bit darker to get some wood. Tara then."

Jean and I arrived back home with our war surplus treasure.

Lucy greeted us with excitement. "Oh, what lovely girls you are." If Dad said the hand grenades were safe Mum wouldn't argue with him. She trusted his judgment on the matter.

We came in from the freezing cold with two shopping bags full of grenades. After we piled some onto the fire it was a lovely big flame.

Lucy kissed our cheeks. "Tonight it's not just one old shoe burning. Oh this is sheer heaven."

Herby took a shovel full of embers from the fire into the kitchen and carried it up to our bedroom fireplace.

"Sheer luxury!" He exclaimed.

We quickly slid under the coats on the beds sticking legs into the sleeves so they wouldn't fall off.

Herby said, "Well yers are all spoilt rotten tonight."

We dozed off, feeling like royalty, having fire in the bedroom for a few hours. We often broke off icicles from the windows to drink at bedtime, but not tonight. Our lovely warm room had its own fire, the first one ever.

We burned the grenades every night for a month with only an occasional hissing and crackling sound. One night, the fire suddenly exploded out onto the hearth.

Mum became hysterical, thinking we would all be blown to bits. Herbert calmly shoveled the embers back into the grate, and we went back to reading our library books, as if it was perfectly normal.

I'm sure we could have been hurt if one of the grenades been dry and still active. I think when you're dirt poor God looks after you even if you are burning hand grenades to stop yourself from freezing to death.

Two old barges were stacked on top of each other at the top of Briarwood Road for years, a great place for kids to play, but probably quite dangerous.

One time my brother Frank fell from the top of

the second barge, and a pole stuck into the side of his head. He was about four-years-old.

We all held onto the pole as we walked him back down to our house. It was quite a sight, my little brother bleeding from his head with a four-foot pole stuck into the side of his skull. Frantic neighbours poured out, quite hysterical at the scene. Being little kids we just took it all as part of our games. Mum had to call an ambulance and little Frank was taken to the children's hospital to have the pole removed.

Another time, Jean and I opened a big box and found two yellow parachutes inside. We dragged them all the way back home and showed our Mum.

"Wow!" Lucy was instantly inspired. "There's enough material here to make you girls lovely twirly skirts." She cut them out and sewed them up on her singer foot-pedal machine. Elastic in the waistbands, we now had bright new outfits. Lucy dyed them green so no one would know they were from pinched parachutes.

We were overjoyed having such lovely twirly

skirts, and we would spin outside, showing off to all the kids on the street how clever Mum was.

The actions of my mother to create such joy for us reflected the many brave women who had to find the inner strength to keep going through poverty and war. Most men were still away in the services even after the war was over.

Every Mum had either knitting needles, a darning needle, or a crochet hook in her hand all day long. They multi-tasked to provide food and clothing. Mums in our family could all sew and would buy the kids adult coats from rummage sales. Then they'd cut them down and adjust them to fit us.

Lucy tailored everyone costumes for a local dance class recital. She was paid pennies for all the work involved.

When the church advertised a rummage sale, Lucy was in front of the building hours before it opened. She found adult coats and outfits to trim down. She made us all a winter coat each. Otherwise we relied on the convent on Princess Road for a free used coat.

At one rummage sale, Lucy lifted me up on the table with all the ladies' frocks. She selected one and pulled it over my head.

"I'll put a few darts in here, and a nice hem on it. Then you will look a treat."

I looked over. My Junior Two teacher was behind the counter selling them. My face blushed crimson at the embarrassment of being so poor.

I wasn't even aware until I was sixteen that you could actually buy new clothes in stores. I thought everyone's mum made all their own clothes, except maybe for rich people. The only clothes we ever bought were school uniforms. Lucy even knitted our vests. But she always tried her best for us.

Chapter Twenty Five

National Health Service

The U.K.'s *National Health Service* (NHS) came into operation at midnight on the fourth of July, 1948. It was the first time anywhere in the world that completely free health care was made available on the basis of citizenship, rather than the payment of fees or insurance premiums.

To the poorest people it was like a gift from God. Many suffered for years with illnesses, but were unable to see a doctor, as they couldn't afford to pay. Now the thought of free medicine and care had people sobbing as they waited in the queues to sign up. They finally had some hope.

The service has been beset with problems throughout its lifetime, not least being a perpetual shortage of funding.

Every working person in Britain pays into the NHS, much like American Social Security. It is taken out of wages, pennies compared to what the citizens receive from the NHS.

Having cared for the nation for more than half a century, most Britons considered the NHS to have been an outstanding success. Healthcare used to be a luxury not everyone could afford.

Life in Britain in the 1930s and 40s before the NHS was tough. Every year, thousands died of infectious diseases like pneumonia, meningitis, tuberculosis, diphtheria, and polio. Infant mortality rate, deaths of children before their first birthday, was around 1 in 20. There was little the piecemeal healthcare system of the day could do.

Against such a background, it is difficult to overstate the impact of the introduction of the *National Health Service*. The NHS, for the first time, provided decent healthcare for all, and with the stroke of a pen transformed the lives of millions.

Life expectancy rose. No longer were little children dying from illnesses that had plagued society for decades.

Ambulances picked up seniors to take them for tests. Nurses came out to homes. Helpers came and assisted elderly and disabled people. Free meals were delivered to seniors daily. No one went bankrupt trying to stay alive in Britain.

Chapter Twenty Six

The Washer

L ucy saw an advertisement in the *Liverpool
Echo* back in 1949. The ad was for a shop on
Bold Street in the city center. They offered
credit for the first time ever. Mum took the tram
straight down with me and my two little brothers,
Frank and Michael.

She picked up the credit application, but she
had to get my Dad to sign for it and return it to the
shop. She hoped they would give her a new washing
machine.

The salesman drove over to our house the next
day to pick up the credit application my Dad had
signed. The skin of Mum's hands was rubbed raw from
scrubbing clothes on a scrub board in the backyard.

Lucy was determined that if she could buy the washing machine then she could take in laundry to pay it off. The loan payment was 10 shillings a week.

After a two-week wait, the application was approved. On a Thursday afternoon, the men delivered a brand new machine with rollers on top and a massive tub and agitator. Everyone in the neighborhood became excited. Mum was the first on Briarwood to have such a luxury item.

All the next week, Jean and I were sent around to knock on doors, especially the neighbours who had babies. We asked them if they would like our Mum to wash their nappies for half a crown.

Soon the washing machine was running all day long until very late in the night. Once the nappies were washed and rung dry, we two sisters would deliver them around the neighborhood, before and after school.

This extra money helped out tremendously.

One day we got a new customer. Everyone used to call her "dirty" Mrs. Roberts because her windows were never cleaned and her house was exceptionally sloppy.

We collected her dirty nappies in a basket and took them home as usual. Mum opened up the first one. It still had the baby's poop in it.

Lucy was outraged. "Who does she think I am? Take these back to the dirty cow. Tell her to rinse them off or wash them her bloody self."

We trudged back to Mrs. Roberts' door. I rang the doorbell. She answered straight away.

I told her, "Excuse me, Mrs. Roberts, can you please rinse these off, me Mum said."

"I'll wash them me bloody self!" she replied, taking them back and slamming the door.

We returned home and relayed the story to Mum. After that incident, we wrote a little slip to each customer, *'Please rinse nappies.'* Our laundry business moved forward with no other incidents.

As well as finding ways to make extra money, Scouser women were creative in clothing their kids. Some taught sewing or knitting for a few bob. Others

taught typing. Mums knitted baby clothes for a
shilling a ball.

Chapter Twenty Seven

Mike's Birth

Aunty Eil whispered, "Shhhhhhhh! Your Mum isn't well." We heard Mum moaning from her bedroom. We were terrified.

Our neighbour Mary Roberts spoke quietly in the back hallway. "It's not good. The baby is folded in half." She told Herby about the complications, as he paced back and forth. The midwife had still not arrived.

"Should we try for another midwife?" he asked Mary.

The woman they had scheduled was off delivering another baby. Us kids didn't know any of this. We had no idea where babies came from and thought the midwife brought them in her bag.

Mum's groans and wails continued for hours. Occasionally someone would look in on us and say, "Go to sleep. Your Mum's not feeling well."

But I couldn't sleep. The suffering went on all night long. My poor Mum was in agony trying to deliver a full breach baby with only neighbors and my Dad.

Finally Dad decided to get a doctor. This was unusual for the time as the midwives handled birthing problems.

Mary Roberts went and called for help. Mary, who had courageously delivered me in 1943, had tried to bring our Mike into the world. Unable to get him turned around, due to his position, she convinced the doctor it was a true emergency. So he followed her back in and took over.

How they managed to unfold Mike and deliver him feet forward was a miracle. He had his umbilical cord wrapped around his throat, and he was blue from lack of oxygen. But he was alive. We heard him cry.

The doctor had brought over our new baby. We

didn't know he had cut a large incision in my Mum to allow Mike's feet to escape.

She should have been in hospital. They should have seen something odd on her final maternity visit, but none of that happened. Although she had been given an internal exam a week prior no one noticed the baby was full breach.

Mum now had four little kids to feed every day. Back then, most families had at least five kids—no birth control pills yet—so the methods they used tended to fail.

When our Mike was little, he often suffered convulsions caused from the lack of oxygen at his birth. After Michael came into the world in 1949, he had lots of medical problems. Terrible convulsions sometimes lasted for hours.

Lucy would sob uncontrollably, hold him in her arms, and try to rock him to sleep. No one knew what to do for him. Finally, Lucy cried all the time. With the other kids fighting constantly and Michael having so many health problems, it was too much for Mum to cope.

One morning, Lucy refused to get out of bed. Herbert didn't know what to do, so he asked Mrs. Davis across the street if he could use her telephone. Herbert rang Eileen, Lucy's big sister, and he explained what was going on.

Eileen rushed over as fast as she could run, with her little ones in tow. Nell came along with her.

When the women arrived, I wanted to tell my Mum that my brother had taken my colouring book. This was a huge problem I thought. Mum waved her arms at me and said, "Not now love. Not now."

My Aunty Eileen ushered me downstairs and asked me to be a good girl and stay quiet. Pretty soon Doctor Roberts arrived, and he told Dad, "Your wife is having a nervous breakdown. Its all too much for her to manage. She needs to go away for six weeks complete rest."

Mum was then sent away to a Catholic convalescence home in the south of England. We were devastated at being on our own for the first time. Dad

went to ask for help from the church. The Nuns
immediately sprang into action and helped us get by
without our Mum. We had Nuns come every day to get
us ready for School, help us with homework, and keep
order. No more fighting.

We were all given lovely dinners each night,
something we never had prior. It was an amazing
time. The Nuns who cared for us were wonderful
people. One sister sticks in my memory, as the kindest
person I have ever met. Her name was Sister
Josephine. She helped buy some of the books I needed
to study for my 11 plus exam.

This was the only chance for a decent
education. Sister Josephine managed to provide me
about $1/3^{rd}$ of the books I needed.

On the day of the exam, I had never heard of
two-thirds of the questions. So, I failed. I felt so badly,
as I knew sister Josephine had tried to improve my life.

Mum phoned us once a week from the
convalescence home. Mrs. Davis had a phone, across
the street. Mrs. Davis was so kind she allowed us to use

her phone for incoming and outgoing calls.

Dad warned me not to mention any mean things that our brothers or Jean had done. We weren't to upset Lucy.

Six weeks was an eternity to us kids. Mum returned home to Liverpool. She brought us each a little present from the rummage sale held at the convalescence facility. Lucy gave Jean and I our first two-piece bathing suits. Mine was a lovely purple and green, ruched fitted top and pull-up bottom, I absolutely loved it.

Jean's suit was pink and red, in the same style with a ruched top and bottom. We felt like film stars in them. Plus they were terrific bargains at six-pence each.

I studied for eight years when my children were small, to educate myself for a better chance in life. I remembered Sister Josephine's advice.

"Educated people do so much better," she had told me when I was 11.

On Mum's first Sunday back home, we all

headed down to the"Prom" in Aigburth. The Prom was a lovely scenic walk along the River Mersey with flower beds and lots of activities. There were football matches on a lovely sunny day. Jean and I wore our new two-piece bathing suits, and we splashed each other in the river, climbing up on rocks and feeling so happy.

While Lucy recovered, Dad was a lot more helpful. I think Doctor Roberts advised him to pitch in. Back then, the men lived like kings, while the women did 90% of the housework.

Lucy eventually found a job in the *Tizer* factory, which was a local bottling plant that made soda pop. She stood all day for eight hours on a conveyor belt, where she stuck labels onto bottles. A grueling job, but she was much happier after she made nice friends there.

Life Improved for all of us having extra money that Mum earned with her hard work. Mum coped so much better now, after we all pitched in at the house. As soon as we grew, each one of us could shop, cook, wash and iron clothes, and clean the whole house. By our teenage years we could all easily feed and clothe a family of seven.

Chapter Twenty Eight

The Steering Cart

Me Dad arrived home from work one Friday night carrying wood planks.

Lucy greeted him. "Whats that for love?"

"Well I'm going to make these kids a smashing steering cart," he said. "I got these from the rubbish at work. Ideal to make it. I just need some wheels."

Herby spent the next two weeks building that steering cart. He found wheels from an old scooter and a little kids' discarded bike. He attached a long handle so we could pull it.

We could hardly contain our excitement on receiving such a smashing cart to ride on. We had no idea why he had made it in the first place.

Construction had started on numerous new houses, right across the road from us. Dad was busy drawing up plans, but we had no idea what they were for. When the whistle blew on Monday, to knock off work at the construction site, Dad handed us a list.

"Do, you get ten red bricks," he told me. "Jean, ten grey. Frank, ten multi-coloured. Stack them onto the steering cart, cover them up with this old blanket, and pull them back home."

Us kids were so amused about such an important job that it was all a fun game.

Dad then stretched strings in our backyard and dug trenches for the footing. It took us almost a year of trips back and forth to supply the b ricks for a double course. Eventually, he built us a smashing back kitchen, which still stands today.

Herby spent his next five years inventing a quilting machine in the little back kitchen he had erected with his own two hands. He spent endless hours with library books studying engines, motors, and the mechanics of how they worked. He sketched ideas onto paper and then cut out the shapes from sheet metal, with only hand tools. Dad refined his homemade parts to his specific design.

What wonderful days we lived back then.

My Dad, Herby Doyle still playing in1985 | credit: Doreen Doyle

The few-thousand pounds that Herby made from his company for inventing the quilting machine provided a deposit on a three-bedroom house with a bathroom inside and—best of all—running hot water. We took such lovely baths now.

All our friends from Briarwood Road came over to see our new house. Most visitors were amazed at the steaming water coming straight out the tap.

We ripped up the old linoleum floor and kept the fire going 24/7, as the water tank sat behind the fire. It provided for deep baths. We were overjoyed, living the life of luxury.

I had no idea that we were very poor, as everyone near to us was also in the same position. This continued after the war. My Dad used to convince us that we were quite wealthy.

As we shared our *Oxo* broth dinners, he would say, "By God you kids are spoiled rotten. Some kids are going to bed with no tea. Here you are with a lovely cup of *Oxo* and loads of bread. Plus a gorgeous rice pud your Mum has for afters."

So, I thought, *Wow, we must be very lucky.*

One night, my Dad returned home from work with two hot-water bottles in bags hanging on each handlebar of his bike.

"Father Christmas stopped by my job today," he announced.

"Did he now?" said Mum.

"Yes, he did, and he dropped these lovely hot water bottles off for our Jean and Do."

We were speechless.

Mum filled them up with boiling water from the kettle and wrapped a towel around each. We couldn't believe our luck as we carried them up to our beds, which were covered in old coats from rummage sales. We slid the bottles underneath.

I tucked my legs into the sleeve of the coat that kept me warm at night. I loved my Dad's old Army jacket.

Dad was always pointing out how lucky we were that Father Christmas came to his job and delivered the luxurious hot water bottles. We usually received a new book, or a pencil and sharpener, or sometimes colored pencils and a coloring book. We were convinced that we were "ruined."

At Christmas, Herby would say, "Most kids only hang up a little stocking. You lot hang up pillowcases."

I still recall the absolute joy of those Christmas mornings so many decades ago.

Chapter Twenty Nine

The Windfalls

T he children of Liverpool's working classes were hungry all the time just after World War Two.

One day, my big sister Jean overheard some kids discussing a house on Carnatic Drive. This place had tennis courts and an apple orchard. The kindly people allowed neighbourhood kids to gather up apple windfalls for free.

"Wow!" said Jean. "I 'ave to tell me Mum."

All the cousins and Lucy's Sisters came over on Saturday, along with Gladys and her children. Once they arrived we told them about the amazing place Jean had heard about. It was only one street over from Briarwood Road.

The Mums held a meeting and agreed.

"Okay. You can all go. But be polite. And don't be too greedy."

"Can we take our Mike?" said Jean. He was in a nice deep pram.

"Okay," said Mum. "Be back in an hour or so."

Doreen, Jean, and Frank 1945 | credit: Doreen Doyle

Off we went, all the kids, to locate the house with the apple trees. We walked up every driveway until we saw the tennis court and the adjacent orchard.

Jean said, "This must be the right place. Come on you lot."

Up the drive we all walked in our tattered homemade clothes. A young man was washing a fancy sports car in the driveway.

"Hello!" he exclaimed. "May I help you?"

Jean stepped forward as usual.

"Excuse me, mister," she said. "Do you have any windfalls we could possibly have, please?"

He smirked and said, "I'll be right back."

Two very posh, well-dressed older ladies stepped out of the double-front doors.

The man said, "Can you please repeat that for Mummy?"

We knew that he thought we were cute. So Jean asked again even more humbly.

"Why certainly," the Mum said. "How adorable," she told her friend, in her upper-crust accent. They sounded far different from us little Scouser sisters.

"Just don't break any branches, children!" she

shouted after us.

"Oh no, we won't," I answered. "Thank you very much, Mrs."

We pushed Michael's massive pram to the gate of the orchard.

Jean took charge of the apple operation. "Get our Mike out. We'll fill up the pram. Look they 'ave tons of 'em everywhere."

We stuck our Mike to crawl around on his own. He kept busy while we all grabbed up the fallen apples. In no time at all, we filled up the deep pram. Then we started stuffing apples in our jumpers, knickers, pants, everywhere.

We placed baby Mike back on top of the pram cover, holding his arms so he wouldn't fall off the pile. We cousins hauled back loads of apples. As we turned the corner onto Briarwood Road, the neighbors noticed us.

"Where did yer get those?" asked Mary Brown.

"None of yer business," Jean retorted. "Come on gang. Don't talk to any of them."

By now, half a dozen kids had popped out to spectate.

"Keep it secret or they'll go and ruin it for us," Jean whispered.

We delivered our first load of apples home to the Mums. These were divided up evenly for each family. None of us kids ever had our own piece of fruit, except at Christmas time. So it was beyond our wildest dreams eating all those apples.

Lucy baked apple pies for us as well as an apple crumble. We sat patiently waiting to taste the gorgeous apple crumble. Mum had managed to make custard to coat on top, from the free dried milk, so it was a treat beyond our wildest imaginings that day. The aroma of the flaky crust made us dizzy with anticipation. We had afters every day for a week. That made us so happy.

We returned to the orchard every single week that autumn and repeated the big apple haul. It was so wonderful, and it lasted until the winter when there were no more windfalls to take.

Then we were back to plum jam on bread toasted by the fire. It was the best treat our Mum could afford in those days. Strawberry jam was much more expensive than the plum jam for some reason. We used to buy the massive two-pound jars at the local shop. The plum jam was an unknown brand name. So, of course, it was more affordable.

Our Mums always found ways to get us treats by taking on extra work. Lucy often sewed costumes for the local dancing school, which held their lessons every Friday in the *People's Hall* basement. It featured a piano and a small stage. So, it was the ideal place to learn tap dance and beginner ballet.

All the little girls enrolled. After many pleadings, somehow Lucy came up with the shilling a week for us to attend. Jean and I absolutely loved our dance lessons. All our best mates attended: Joan Sargent, Mary Roberts, Lynne Roberts, and Cynthia Green, who was the best dancer in the entire troupe.

For hours every day, Lucy sewed custom costumes for each girl to wear on the night of the big recital. It was held in *Sudley Road School* in Aigburth Vale. They had a proper massive hall and stage.

Just before the night of the show, our Frank became ill with the measles. Mum stayed home with him. Our neighbor Mrs. Sargent offered to take me and Jean to the recital with her daughter Joan, who was in the chorus with me. We were fairies in white tutus and satin tops.

Mum managed to sew my costume with all the tiny scrap pieces left over from the other kids' material. She was so clever. You could hardly see the multiple seams joining it all together. Without her skills we could never have attended the recital.

It was such an exciting evening, very rare for us to be at such a massive show. We were ushered into the stairwell to wait our turns and head up on stage.

Cynthia Green was the star of *Sleeping Beauty*, and she danced so lovely. She was dirt poor like us, with welly marks round her legs. We all wore wellies in the winter and pumps in the summer. The wellies rubbed the skin off our bare legs until they had scabs on them, and it made it very hard to walk to and from school.

Gillian my cousin, Jean, Frank Me, Nana, and Mike,
Briarwood Road 1951 | Doreen Doyle

After Cynthia finished her beautiful dance performance, we were brought out of the freezing stairwell and onto the stage. I was shivering uncontrollably. We did our little dance, and then we waited for the grand finalé.

As I walked back home I felt quite ill.

Mrs. Sargent felt my head.

"Oh Lord," she said. "Your Mum's going to have her hands full."

Snow began to fall on us. Joan and my Sister Jean squealed with delight and ran off ahead of us to slide in the slick snow.

As we approached home, I couldn't walk any farther. Mrs. Sargent picked me up over her shoulder and carried me inside.

My poor Mum was devastated when she saw me so ill. Lucy was such an emotional Mum, and she often cried if one of us got hurt or became sick.

I lay bedridden for over a week with the measles, then tonsillitis followed. I still remember my Mum smoothing out my pillow. My temperature was so high that I kept seeing lumps on the pillow that maybe weren't even there.

After two weeks, though, I completely recovered, and life went back to usual.

Chapter Thirty

The Carol Singers

A t Christmas time some of us kids headed out into the neighbourhood to sing carols. We took our little Michael who was now nine-months-old to give my Mum a break. Mike had curly black hair and big blue eyes. So, we knew he would help make us some money. Plus Mum was grateful for the break.

Joan Sargent, Janet Ferguson, and Mary Brown had been out singing since September. Instead of a penny, sometimes they would make six-pence or even a shilling. Word quickly spread around the impoverished children on Briarwood.

Lucy wrote up a list of supplies we needed for Christmas dinner, as did Gladys and Eileen. Nell was cared for, as her Mam and Mad helped her out. But it was difficult for us to afford it all.

One Saturday afternoon, Eileen and Gladys arrived at our house with all their kids. We cousins decided it would be a smashing idea if we headed out carol singing. The Mums agreed, especially when they heard of the money we might make singing.

We left as soon as it got dark. First, we knocked to ask if we could sing. Once the family agreed, we sang four or five carols. Then we rang the bell to hopefully receive some payment. Everyone already knew us. So, most people gladly gave a few pennies. We sang our hearts out for hours.

When we returned home, shivering from the frigid night, our Mums sorted out all the change that we'd received.

Lucy announced, "We 'ave enough to get some fruit."

"Yeah!" We all shouted.

"We 'ave enough for a nice Christmas cake too," Gladys added.

We kids cheered.

"And decorations," Eileen said.

We were beside ourselves with excitement.

Our Mums, emboldened by the sight of all that cash, asked us if we wanted to go out again!

We agreed, apart from little Gladys and little Frank, who were too tired by now.

"Go up Gladeville Road this time," said Mum, "and we will 'ave some nice hot cocoa ready for yah when you come home."

We marched over to Gladeville Road and sang for the neighborhood for several more hours. When we returned home, the Mums again counted the pile of change.

Lucy said, "Enough for some cheese and crackers."

Aunty Eileen added, "Tangerines fer us."

The Mums crossed off items from their shopping lists. We had welly marks around our little legs and were frozen purple.

The Mums prepared bowls of hot water to

warm our feet. All us kids felt so empowered by the money we made from carol singing. The total was under seven pounds, but an absolute fortune for us. This was my happiest Christmas ever, 1949. None of us, when we became adults, remembered a single Christmas gift we had ever received as children, but we all remembered that most lovely celebration, the one we had sung to make a success.

From having absolutely nothing to enjoying a small chicken with sage and onion stuffing, and fruit, nuts, and a real Christmas cake with marzipan, it was our most fantastic Christmas dinner ever. I can still remember the lovely smells of delicious food cooking that day. Chicken in the oven, roasties browning as they cooked, our tummies rumbled all morning in anticipation of the wonderful feast we had all provided.

We kids even enjoyed a glass of sherry with lemonade or port wine. They were in cracked cups from *Ray's* sale, but we were living like royalty that bitter winter of 1949. Mum and Dad toasted to us children for all our hard work, out singing for hours, and against all the odds, providing that wonderful Christmas dinner. This was my best Christmas memory ever.

Chapter Thirty One

1950's

I attended Catholic School and used to go to confession with our class once each week. But one of the priests was a pedophile. As an innocent child I didn't understand at first. He asked me the most disgusting questions in the confessional booth. I heard his vestments rustling as he masturbated under his robe each time.

"Do you let boys put their fingers into your private?" he said.

I was petrified. I never heard of anything like that in my life. I was only seven-years-old. Terrified, I avoided him as much as possible.

If we had a school play, the priest would walk right into our dressing room as we were changing. I

had only just begun to wear a bra. I was 13-years-old
and very shy. When he barged in, I was so scared
trying to cover up my knickers and bra with my
sweater.

This priest stood there masturbating under his
robes next to the headmistress and two of the
teachers. They seemed completely oblivious to what
was going on.

One time, this priest walked over to me and
stroked his hand down my back, putting his finger
into the crack of my bum. I froze in terror.

I couldn't wait to tell my Mum, who, to my
surprise, assumed he had accidentally done that, *being
a man of God.*

"He isn't a man of God! Mum, he is a sicko!" I
screamed at her.

Nothing was done about this terrible priest. He
carried on his torment of all the young girls at the
school.

Years later, when I worked at *Dista Products* up
in Speke, I met Marjorie, a friend of my cousin Eileen.

We began to discuss our school, which she had also attended years earlier.

"Did you ever go to confession with the head Priest" she asked me.

"Yes, I did. Sicko comes to mind."

She knew, and she told me her story of how he had also asked her disgusting questions. She left his confessional in tears, afraid of him.

No one ever forced the issue or told the police, like they should have done.

It's hard to imagine a man like that priest with so much power over all those innocent little girls. Luckily, I managed to avoid him as I grew older.

But still, the church played a large part in our lives. We made our first confessions then went onto Holy Communion. Mum had no money to buy me a Communion dress. The other girls in my class raved about gorgeous dresses that their Mums had bought for them.

When I mentioned this to my Mum she bought me a green silk ladies' dress in the rummage sale for six-pence.

"Don't worry, darlin'," she said. "When I'm done with this you will look an absolute treat."

Lucy tried every trick she knew to turn the green dress white. She bleached it for days, boiled it, soaked it in blue stuff, but the best it came out was a dull yellow.

She altered it to fit me and pressed it carefully. Then I tried it on.

"What do you think, my love?" she asked.

I would never hurt Mum's feelings after all of her hard work. "I absolutely love it," I said as I watched her beaming face.

As I walked in the procession, some of the richer Mums gave me sympathetic looks, but I held my head high, so proud of my Mum's heroic efforts with six-pence and sheer determination. She made my Holy Communion dress from unconditional love. I have never forgotten that day.

The church and school would help us 'poor kids' in other ways. Each year our school arranged a

day trip on a Charabang. The Charabang was a regular
coach style bus. We used to sing a song on the way.

"We all went on a Charrabang; We all went on a
Charrabang; charra charra charra bang bang bang…"

The song lasted for 20 minutes at least. Some of
the school kids would add naughty words.

At the end, they sang, "And now we're going to
finish it; finny finny finny shit shit shit!"

Trips were so much fun. We looked forward for
months. Usually these were to Rhyl, Blackpool, or
some other holiday destination. We were treated to
fish and chips for tea at a convent. They even gave
each child one shilling to spend.

I spent mine on two bars of rock which they
sold in all the beach towns. I brought them home for
my brothers and my sister to share, as they hadn't
been able to go on the trip.

Mum grabbed me by my cheeks and said,
"Whoever gets you will be the luckiest man in the
world."

I loved being complimented on my kindness.

During the 1950s, us Scousers struggled to get by, but we enjoyed lots of lovely times as well. At family gatherings we played cards, *Chutes and Ladders*, and had singalongs with my Dad playing his guitar. All the Aunties and Cousins sang too. We knew every song inside and out, all the hits from the 40s and early 50s.

Mum and Dad had lovely voices. We kids inherited good singing voices too. It was such an enjoyable time, and I miss those lovely singalongs.

Our house had only a sideboard and a sewing machine in the front living room. One sunny Saturday morning, my Uncle Tom showed up in a big truck.

"Do you have ten bob, Lu?" he asked Mum.

Mum went through her bag and pulled out 10 shillings. Uncle Tom went back outside and returned with his mate, carrying a gorgeous white two-seater couch. Then they delivered an easy chair.

"Is it okay here, Lu?" he asked.

"It's not pinched, is it, Tom?" Mum asked him, all serious.

"Naah. It fell off the back of a truck, love."

"Oh. Thank goodness." My lovely gullible mum went a long. I think she actually believed her brother.

As a little girl, I knew it was pinched from somewhere, but the times were hard, so he was doing what he saw as a good deed.

We felt like royalty with our new posh sitting room furniture.

Chapter Thirty Two

First Holiday

When I was thirteen, my Uncle Jack Whitney invited me down to London for a week's holiday. This was the very first holiday I ever took. Mum accompanied me to Lime Street station to catch the train by myself. She was so nervous to let me go alone that she climbed aboard the train and introduced herself and me to everyone on board.

I blushed, as she asked the passengers to please make sure I was safe on the journey and to look out for me. Of course, they all willingly adopted me, and they promised Lucy I would be safe. She hugged them all. That was Mum.

What a fantastic week at Uncle Jack and Aunty

Joyce's house with my two cousins, Eileen and David. Every day they took us out to the beach, a different one each time. We walked for miles up the cliffs and ate our meals at cafés, eggs and chips. I felt like I'd been whisked away to heaven.

Jack Whitney and his bride Joyce | credit: Peter Whitney

Lucy coached me to make sure I volunteered to iron and clean, and also pay Aunty Joyce two pound for my keep. Aunty Joyce refused to take the money.

"You keep it love," she said, "so you have something to spend."

I couldn't believe my luck. I'd arrived with no spending money and usually got just six pence a week for my allowance. So, two pounds was a fortune. I bought gifts to bring home for everyone.

When I was packing my clothes to return to Liverpool, Uncle Jack got emotional and said, "I'm going with her, love. She's only a little girl. It's a long trip by herself."

I was so excited. My favorite Uncle traveled all the way back to Liverpool with me, just to make sure I was okay.

Chapter Thirty Three

Going to America

T he next place our family lived was at the *People's Hall* in Aigburth Vale. This move is the reason that I eventually emigrated to the U.S. We were caretakers for the *Hall*. Our family catered weddings and other social functions. It was a huge building with billiard halls and a dance studio in the basement, with a stage and piano. This is where we had attended dance classes there-years earlier.

Neither one of my parents had any training in running such a place. Dad was in charge of keeping the bowling greens perfect and cleaning the facility.

We ran the place for two years before my parents went bankrupt. They had no cash register. So, a lot of people would steal out of the drawer that they kept the money in. It could have been a pretty lucrative business if either one of them knew how to run it properly.

There was a counter where we sold an assortment of goods: *Eccles* cakes, tea,and coffee, and breakfasts for the local factory workers.

Each morning, I prepared loads of take-out breakfasts for the *Tizer* factory just down the street. Bacon and egg on toast and other standards, I worked early until 8:45am. Then I had to run to school on Aigburth Road.

After school, I returned to work in the *Hall* until 11pm when we closed. My sister worked during the day shift.

Every Friday night, the *Merseyside Wheelers*, a cycling club, came into the *Hall*. I listened to their stories of weekend bikers and the many trips they all took together. I saved up a deposit and bought myself a lovely blue and black *Dayton* 5-speed bike. I soon joined the *Wheelers* and met up with them every Sunday morning to ride the ferry across the Mersey to Birkenhead. Then we all rode off to North Wales.

I wasn't as good a cyclist as most of them. So when we reached our first stop in Queensferry I was usually done for and opted to hang out there with a few of the other girls.

At fourteen -years-old and very proud of myself riding my bike so far, occasionally I would go as far as Rhyl in Wales a good 30 plus miles away. Even in the winter we would go on "holly runs" to find wild holly and bring it back to Liverpool to decorate for Christmas.

One day I was sitting in *Bazz's* café when in walked a Greek God, a tall blond fella with a motorcycle and huge muscles. I was smitten, but he was never interested in me.

When I heard he was getting married I decided to follow up on an advert I had seen in the Liverpool *Echo:*

"Come to America. Babysit little kids. Sit on a beach all day, and sometimes they even give you a car."

That sounded like absolute heaven. I was now working in *Dista Products* in Speke from 7:30am until 4:30 pm. Then at the *Mayfair* on Aigburth Road from 5pm til 11pm—six days a week.

I applied to be an English Nanny and was accepted by a New Jersey family.

Mum and Dad were highly upset, but I kept promising them I would only be gone one year. At the end of this term, the family had agreed to pay for your air fare home. So, they both reluctantly signed the release form for me to leave and enter a binding contract.

I left Speke Airport on my first plane ride on the 21st of March, 1963, full of anticipation. I had to wait inside London Airport for ten hours to catch the next flight to JFK Airport in New York City.

When I left England I was nineteen. I arrived at New York completely exhausted, as it was 3am our time. There I met four other English girls coming to work as nannies. We were warned not to talk to anyone unless they were the people sent to meet us. This spooked us, and we wondered what dangers there could be waiting.

In the airport terminal, a man and woman approached us and asked, "Is one of you girls Doreen Doyle?"

I was so relieved. "Yeah, I am."

The girl waiting beside me began to cry. I felt so sorry for her, but I couldn't stay.

"Don't worry, love," I said. "You'll be okay. Someone will be here for you soon."

The woman who came to pick me up asked, "What language was that you were just talking?"

I couldn't believe the question.

She thought, with my thick Scouse accent, that I was speaking a foreign language.

So, I answered, "Gaelic." I thought this might prove to be a help later on.

The next day, that woman, my boss, announced to her ladies' group, "She actually speaks Gaelic and takes a shower every day. And yes I think they are her own teeth."

I was standing right there, and I had never been so insulted in my life. These women with their two sets of false eyelashes and glued-on fingernails were discussing me like I was a prize racehorse.

I was hired as the children's Nanny, but my boss liked to dress me up as an English maid in a uniform to impress her friends. At first I believed all Americans must be like this group.

"I want you to serve my best friends as politely as you can," she said. "One has a French maid, but I want to show them you."

I was livid, although I smiled sweetly and did as I was told. This woman thought she owned me, because I had come to work for her.

One of the women asked me, "Have you ever seen a steak as big as here?" I was serving them.

"Yes," I said. "We have cows in England." I thought to myself *you stupid mare.* Of course, we could never eat a half-pound steak. That would have fed the whole family! I was amazed how ignorant these women were.

"Do you have running hot water over there?" asked the other one.

This continued until it was time to serve them coffee. I was much disgusted with them, so I have to admit I overfilled double eyelashes' cup and it spilled all over her.

"I'm so dreadfully sorry. Did that get onto your lovely skirt? Oh dear me." I said in my poshest accent. I was never asked to serve coffee again to her snobby friends.

I was a true Scouser girl.

This year I spent with that New Jersey family was the worst one I ever had. I was hired to care for the children, not to be a 24-hour maid. I wasn't even fed on my day off. But I kept silent as I knew my parents couldn't afford to save me and pay off my contract, let alone the air fare to return to England.

In the final two months, the wife tried every trick in the book to make me answer her back, so she wouldn't have to pay my plane fare.

I was too smart for her.

If I came in late on my day off, she would demand I clean the kitchen and wash the floor before going to bed.

"Sure." I said. "Would you like me to vacuum as well?"

No way was I going to be left stranded in America without my fare home. Some of my friends were thrown out in the streets by these families. The British Consulate advised them to write to the newspapers when they returned home. We all did.

My friend Anne was the luckiest out of the five Nannies I knew. Her boss was lovely. She had five little kids.

When Anne's boss heard we weren't being fed on our days off, she made us breakfast buffets. Every week, we had a feast with bacon and eggs, pancakes and more. She was such a wonderful lady.

My Gaelic scheme worked out very well. If we met each other we would just speak quickly using our own expressions. We'd say, "Look at the gob on that cracked cow. Her double set of flutterers don't help. Only a gob a mudda could love." We would double up laughing.

"What's so funny, Doreen?" my boss asked.

"My friend Angela keeps telling me Gaelic jokes."

The ladies sat smiling up at us, happy to brag that we were bilingual.

On my first Christmas away from home, my boss woke me up and said, "I know it's a holiday, so just lightly dust and vacuum today."

I was so choked up I couldn't answer. I wanted so badly to be home with my family. They tried for hours to get through on the phone, but back then it was difficult to place a phone call on a holiday. I cried as I vacuumed the living room. That's when the doorbell rang.

"Get that, Doreen!" my boss screamed over the noise of the vacuum.

It was her neighbor Leatrice, holding a little radio for me. She hugged me. More importantly, she said, "Happy Christmas, Doreen."

I sobbed.

"Shhh," she said. "You'll be home in no time, sweetheart."

Leatrice's kindness that day stuck with me. I realized then that not all Americans were like my boss. There were some wonderfully kind ones, and that has proven true as I've gone through my long journey. With no family here, I have found caring friends who have helped me every step of the way.

I have no regrets about emigrating to America even though I didn't intend to.

After three months in the U.S., I met Joe. He was quite the character, and he was absolutely smitten with me from day one, sending huge bouquets of flowers after each date.

"I'm not staying," I told him. "I'm going back after my year is up."

I did return to Liverpool as I'd promised my parents, but I also realized that I loved Joe. So, I had the hard job of telling my Mum and Dad, Lucy and Herby, that I was leaving them for good.

Doreen and Hubby Joe, Christmas 2015 | credit: Joe Giambrone

Joe and I were married on the 15th of May, 1965. I lost Joe on the 5th of August, 2017, during the writing of this memoir. We had all 52 years of happiness, sadness, anger (much!) and love. I would not trade it for anything.

Chapter Thirty Four

Epilogue

L iverpool's bombed-out streets remained an eyesore until the 1960s, when they were rebuilt with houses on most of them.

This book has shown the terrible sacrifices those past generations made in order to ensure that the spirit of the British people would never be broken. They are never to be forgotten.

The *Ernest Brown Junior Instructional Centre* tragedy left a lasting impression on the Liverpool community. It became known as the *"Durning Road Bombing."* In 2001, the local church of St. Cyprian and its congregation erected a war memorial in honor of those who had perished there. A glass plaque contains 150 names of those who died. This was mounted inside the church. The church has since closed, and

the memorial was moved to storage in the Anglican
Cathedral.

Due to the work of local people, that memorial
has now been re-erected at *Kensington Junior School* on
Brae Street, very close to where the *Ernest Brown
Junior Instructional Centre* once stood.

My two Uncles, Tom and Jack Whitney, had to
celebrate every time they met up for the rest of their
lives, toasting one another with pints until both were
plastered. Half the pub usually joined in after hearing
their many war stories.

Jack Whitney married Joyce as soon as he
returned to London. They were both still eighteen-
years old. Jack moved south, but whenever he came
home to Liverpool for a visit he would give every kid
in the family half a crown each, an absolute fortune.
We never received anything from any other family
members, but somehow Uncle Jack managed to do
this.

He also brought us little cousins to see our very
first film at the Mayfair. He knew how poor we were,

and how much it meant to be treated to a movie. Uncle Jack had a heart of gold.

Mike, Frank, and Elaine a month before I emigrated in 1963 | credit Doreen Doyle

Mike Doyle was a lovely brother. I loved him dearly. He saved up for two years to come and visit me in America when he was sixteen-years-old. I still treasure his memory today.

We didn't have much when Mike visited me. Newly married, and my hubby only worked a few days a week, but Mike was happy just to go to a park and take long walks in America. We played cards every day to pass the time. He enjoyed visiting his big Sister. We wrote to each other for many years.

Mike died many years later, sadly. It was an accident, carbon monoxide poisoning caused by a faulty cooker that my Mum had sold to him three months earlier. The pain Lucy suffered because of that tragedy killed her. Four months after my brother Mike died, Lucy Doyle also passed on.

Tom and Gladys Whitney went on to have a total of seven children. They lived at 32 Woodruff Street, Liverpool until the 1960s.

Tom Whitney was born on February 23rd 1912 and died 17th June, 1984. He suffered terribly from his war wounds for the rest of his life. He had seven children: Tommy, born 11th February 1935, died at Smithdown Road Hospital in May of 1937, and also

Peter, Jeanie, Gladys, Barbara, Jimmy & Leslie.

Shelly & Family, Peter Whitney's daughter | credit Peter Whitney

Peter Whitney left Liverpool in 1955 and moved to Swindon after he joined the Army. He married Chris and has two children: Ricky and Shelly. Jeanie married Stan and has three sons. Gladys married Arnfin, a Norwegian, and has one son. Barbara married Joop, a Dutchman, and has two sons.

Jimmy married Peggy and has three sons. Leslie married Carol and has four kids.

Lucy and Herbert Doyle went on to have five of us in total. They are both now deceased. Jean married Eddie and had three kids, Gary, Denise and Suzanne. Gary Hughes, the eldest, died in 2015.

Doreen emigrated to the U.S. in 1963, married Joe and has two kids, Debbi the younger, and Joe, who co-wrote this book. Doreen's husband Joe Giambrone Jr. died in August of 2017.

Frank Doyle married Barbara and had three kids. He is now deceased. Michael Doyle married Ellie and had three kids. Michael is now deceased. Elaine Doyle married Dave and had one son. Dave is deceased, and Elaine also died in August of 2017.

Eileen married Tom Powell. Both are deceased. They had five children. David died as an infant. Eileen married Luiz, who was Portuguese. Luiz is now deceased. They had two kids. Fred married Pat and had two girls. They emigrated to Canada. Tommy married Dot and had two girls. They also emigrated to

Canada. Alan married Shelagh, had three kids and emigrated to Canada.

Jack Whitney married Joyce and moved to London. They had two kids and are both now deceased. Jack Whitney went on to lead a productive life. He worked until he was 62 years old. Sadly, he became a chronic alcoholic and died at the age of 68.

David married, had one girl. Eileen married, had one son. Nellie married Tim O' Sullivan, and both are now deceased. They had three kids. Frank married Freda, had two kids, and emigrated to Canada. June married to Erick, and they had three kids. Larry married to Diane, and they had three kids.

When the war began in 1939, the population of Great Britain was 47,760,000. During the war, 383,800 military and 67,100 civilians were killed, of those 2,716 were from Liverpool, 442 from Birkenhead, 409 from Bootle, 337 from Wallasy.

Tens of thousands were injured during the Blitz, but the joy of having survived helped ease the pain of it all for most Liverpudlians.

Those Scousers were bloody tough stock, and I'm so proud to be one of them. Tara.

Lightning Source UK Ltd.
Milton Keynes UK
UKHW021913161119
353669UK00002B/7/P